Employee Development University(EDU)

Southern California Water Company
A Subsidiary of American States Water Company

The Employee Development University's Vision is *to Empower People to Learn, Change and Grow!*

EDU's Mission Statement

The Employee Development University is an innovative, collaborative organization whose purpose is to provide training and development services to increase employee knowledge, improve skills, and effect positive change in the workplace.

Learning Imperatives

Today's complex and rapidly changing environment demands maximum utilization of a company's number one resource — its people! But, to sustain constant improvement throughout any organization, employees need to enhance their skills and expand their knowledge of new business processes in order to respond more readily to these changes. A well-trained employee can make it easy for an organization to respond and manage change. Formal training programs ensure that the new or the existing employee has the basic knowledge to perform the job satisfactorily.

Corporate University Learning Approach

The Corporate University plays an important role in creating employee development programs aimed at improving productivity and at the same time, encouraging life-long learning among employees. The EDU team holds the belief that learning is a life-long process based on individual motivation, self-directiveness and initiative. The team recognizes the need to design, develop and deliver effective training programs in the most cost-effective manner to meet both the business and employee needs in order to accelerate learning, thereby resulting in benefits to the Company and to the individual. This assurance adds value to the Company and at the same time, guarantees consistency by developing employees on the core business practices.

The Business Communications Course supports one of the Company's educational strategies to *develop a curriculum for each level of management, which leads to development of skills required to meet the business needs.* This course is just *one* approach to ensure that the employees have the requisite skills to succeed in their current or desired positions and to help meet the changing business needs.

Organizational Alignment

The Employee Development University, as a business unit under Customer and Operations Support, is assigned the responsibilities to administer all education and training programs to support the company's mission statement as well as EDU's mission statement. EDU is also organized to support and implement the Business Communications Course through collaborative efforts with such learning partners as Harcourt Brace & Company.

Customer Publication

The Employee Development University team has identified the textbook, *Effective Business Writing* along with the *Harbrace Basic Writer's Workbook* as the cornerstone for the Business Communications Course. Specific chapters of the textbook are incorporated with the Writer's Workbook to give the student both practical and theoretical applications. Through the utilization of the Writer's Workbook, the student will be able to incorporate lessons learned on grammar and vocabulary in reports and business letters. The intended learning objectives are outlined in the course syllabus with a specific aim to build the student's writing proficiency for immediate impact and results at the work place.

One of the advantages for customizing this course is to provide the employees (students) with only what is needed so that they can quickly apply the principles and practices to their work environment. Other supporting materials from Harcourt Brace & Company are combined to meet the course objectives and to give the employee (student) a total learning experience.

"In order for employees to feel empowered about learning, they must become active participants in the process. Evolving beyond the training functions, one of EDU's main goals is to encourage employees to learn how to utilize education as a catalyst for change — to empower people to Learn, Change and Grow!" *Diane D. Rentfrow, Corporate Dean*

Harbrace
Basic Writer's
Workbook

James L. Henderson

 CENGAGE
Learning™

Australia • Brazil • Japan • Korea • Mexico • Singapore • Spain • United Kingdom • United States

CENGAGE
Learning™

Harbrace Basic Writer's Workbook

James L. Henderson

Executive Editors:
Michele Baird

Maureen Staudt

Michael Stranz

Project Development Manager:
Linda deStefano

Senior Marketing Coordinators:
Sara Mercurio

Lindsay Shapiro

Production/Manufacturing Manager:
Donna M. Brown

PreMedia Services Supervisor:
Rebecca A. Walker

Rights & Permissions Specialist:
Kalina Hintz

Cover Image:
Getty Images*

* Unless otherwise noted, all cover images used
by Custom Solutions, a part of Cengage Learning,
have been supplied courtesy of Getty Images with
the exception of the Earthview cover image, which
has been supplied by the National Aeronautics
and Space Administration (NASA).

For product information and technology assistance, contact us at
Cengage Learning Customer & Sales Support, 1-800-354-9706

For permission to use material from this text or product,
submit all requests online at **cengage.com/permissions**
Further permissions questions can be emailed to
permissionrequest@cengage.com

ISBN-13: 978-0-15-58154-3

ISBN-10: 0-15-508154-3

Cengage Learning
5191 Natorp Boulevard
Mason, Ohio 45040
USA

Cengage Learning is a leading provider of customized learning solutions with
office locations around the globe, including Singapore, the United Kingdom,
Australia, Mexico, Brazil, and Japan. Locate your local office at:
international.cengage.com/region

Cengage Learning products are represented in Canada by Nelson Education, Ltd.

For your lifelong learning solutions, visit **custom.cengage.com**

Visit our corporate website at **cengage.com**

Printed in the United States of America

PREFACE

The *Harbrace Basic Writer's Workbook* is designed for students who, for a variety of reasons, may not be prepared to enter a course in first-year composition or another college-level writing course without experiencing a significant level of difficulty. In order to ensure that each of these students has a reasonable chance of success in college-level writing courses some extra preparation might be needed to enhance the level of skills exhibited on college placement tests. The text should also supplement the lack of writing proficiency resulting from incomplete preparation or prolonged absence from the formal classroom setting. Additionally, the lack of reinforcement of learned skills due to personal preoccupation with other, nonacademic situations can be addressed.

The *Harbrace Basic Writer's Workbook* follows the chapter order of the *Harbrace College Handbook, Thirteenth Edition*, and the *Harbrace College Handbook, Brief Thirteenth Edition*, with cross-references to the *Hodges' Harbrace Handbook, Thirteenth Edition*. Exercises cover Chapters 1–28 of the *Harbrace* and 1–32 of the *Hodges*. A student answer key of odd-numbered answers to all the exercises is included at the back of the workbook. This answer key is also cross-referenced to the *Hodges*. The grammatical rules that appear in all three of the handbooks as major headings are repeated in the *Basic Writer's Workbook* with explanations and examples directed toward the student who is, for the most part, unfamiliar with those rules.

The exercises presented in the *Basic Writer's Workbook* are cumulative and require the student to refer frequently to previously covered material in order to effectively approach new material. Students are often required to rewrite entire sentences and paragraphs instead of merely filling in blanks as in objective-type exercises. The exercises are designed to build toward proficiency in writing the short essay after acquiring skills in grammar, sentence construction, and paragraph development.

CONTENTS

CONTENTS

Harcourt Brace & Company

Harcourt Brace & Company

Chapter 1

Sentence Sense

(Hodges 1)

The basic unit of communication in *written* English is the sentence. Notice, we emphasize *written* because, in speaking, we frequently substitute certain grammatical structures with voice inflections, body language, and so on. As you progress in this workbook, you will become acquainted with more levels of sophistication in creating different kinds and styles of sentences.

The English sentence consists of a SUBJECT—a noun or pronoun performing the action or being spoken about; a PREDICATE—the word or group of words that expresses action, an occurrence, or state of being; and a COMPLEMENT— a word that receives the action of the verb, *or* a word that expresses something about the subject.

1a Verbs form the predicate of sentences.

A verb functions as the predicate of a sentence or as an essential part of the predicate. You can recognize a verb by observing its form as well as its function.

WALK! [verb by itself—the subject, "you," is understood]
Marco WALKS. [subject and verb]
Marco WALKS home. [subject, verb, object]
Marco WALKS home quickly. [subject, verb, object, modifier]

A verb can consist of more than one word. The AUXILIARY is often called a *helping verb* or *verb marker*. The verbs *have* and *be* are auxiliaries and follow the pattern of AUXILIARY + VERB. *Can/could*, *may/might*, and *shall/will* follow the same pattern; *can/could* express ability, *may/might* express possibility, and *shall/will* express future tense. (See chapter 7 for a complete discussion of verbs.)

Marco HAD WALKED home.
He WILL BE WALKING later.
He CAN GO now.
He MIGHT STAY longer.

Harcourt Brace & Company

1

Other words might intervene between the auxiliary and the verb.

Marco HAS not GONE yet.

Verbs with prepositions. When verbs are followed by a preposition, they are called phrasal verbs, and mean something different from the verb standing alone. For example, the meaning of *turned* is different from *turned out* or *turned off*. We see this occur also with *look up, burn down, watch out, put off, try on*, and so on. If a phrasal verb has a direct object, the verb and the preposition could be separated. The preposition can come before or after the object.

She *tried* the dress *on* in the store.
She *tried on* the dress in the store.

If the object is a pronoun, the preposition must follow the object.

She *tried* <u>it</u> *on* in the store.

1b Subjects, objects, and complements can be nouns, pronouns, or word groups serving as nouns.

The *subject* is who or what the sentence is about. It can be a noun—

Grace studied hard.

Or a pronoun—

She studied hard.

It can be stated—

You should learn to write well.

Or implied—

(*You*) study!

The subject is usually positioned before the verb—

The *students* are preparing for college.

Except when asking a question—

Are *you* prepared for college?

Or writing an emphatic sentence—

Quite prepared are the *students*.

Or writing a sentence that begins with *it* or *there*—

> *It* is important to prepare for college.
> *There* are good reasons to prepare for college.

Finally, the subject can be simple—

> *Lucy* graduates this year.

Or compound—

> *Lucy* and *Edward* graduate this year.

Complements

Transitive verbs are verbs that denote action and may require a *direct object* to receive or show the result of the action.

> Marcia *bought* books.

If a word is used between the verb and the direct object in order to show to whom or for whom the action occurred, it is called an *indirect object*.

> Marcia bought *John* his books.

Transitive verbs have *voice*, which shows the relationship between the subject and the verb's action. When the subject is performing the action, the verb is in the *active voice*.

> Marcia bought books.

When the subject is receiving the action, the verb is in the *passive voice*.

> The books were bought by Marcia.

Direct and indirect objects, like subjects, can be compound.

> John gave Marie *pencils* and *paper*.
> John gave *Marie* and *Marcia* pencils and paper.

Intransitive verbs do not take direct objects and cannot be made passive. Intransitive verbs refer to, identify, or qualify the subject and help complete the meanings of *be* (*am, is, are, was, were, been*), linking verbs (such as *seem, become*), and sensory verbs (such as *feel, look, smell, sound, taste*).

> John is Marie's *cousin*. (*Cousin* identifies the subject *John*.)
> My lunch became *cold*. (*Cold* describes the subject, *lunch*.)

An *object complement* refers to, identifies, or qualifies the direct object, and helps complete the meaning of verbs such as *make, name, elect, call, paint.*

They named their daughter *Elise.*
Her room was painted *white.*

Verbals

In English, a word's function in a sentence determines what part of speech that word is. Frequently, words that are normally verbs—words that express action, occurrence, or state of being—are used in sentences as nouns, adjectives, or adverbs. When this occurs, we refer to these words as verbals. There are three types of verbals.

Gerunds are verbals as nouns.

He began *shouting.*

Shouting is a gerund and functions as object of the verb *began.*

Learning about verbals is necessary.

Learning is a gerund and functions as subject of the verb *is.*

Participles are verbals used as adjectives.

The *tired* men faced the *howling* wind.

Tired modifies the subject *men,* and *howling* modifies the object *wind.*

Infinitives are verbals used as nouns, adjectives, or adverbs. Infinitives are recognizable by the "to" that usually precedes the verbal. Do not confuse infinitives with prepositional phrases ("to" + noun or pronoun).

As a noun: She didn't want *to drive.*
To drive is an infinitive, object of the verb *want.*

As a noun, omitting "to": We wouldn't dare *refuse* her request.
Refuse is an infinitive, object of the verb [wouldn't] *dare.*

As an adjective: She had no car *to drive.*
To drive is an infinitive modifying the noun *car.*

As an adverb: She was happy *to walk* with us.
To walk is an infinitive, modifying the predicate adjective *happy.*

          Harcourt Brace & Company

1c There are eight classes of words—the parts of speech.

There are eight parts of speech: verbs, nouns, pronouns, adjectives, adverbs, prepositions, conjunctions, and interjections. In an English sentence, a word's function in the sentence determines what part of speech that word is. You shouldn't approach a sentence with the idea that a word's traditional function will be its function all the time. Several years ago, for instance, a famous sports announcer changed a noun to a verb during a football game. When the quarterback calls an "audible," he is changing the next play by changing the signal he calls. The announcer said, "He's audiblizing." The word has become part of the football lexicon as a verb.

The chart shown here provides an overview of parts of speech and their uses in sentences.

PARTS OF SPEECH	FUNCTION IN SENTENCES	EXAMPLES
1. Verbs	Indicate action, occurrence, state of being	Mark *walked* home. He *painted* the house. He *is* tired.
2. Nouns	Subjects and objects	*Marcia* wrote a *story* about college *life*.
3. Pronouns	Substitutes for nouns	*She* will read *it*.
4. Adjectives	Modifiers of nouns and pronouns	The *long* book is *interesting*.
5. Adverbs	Modifiers of verbs, adjectives, other adverbs, or whole clauses	read *easily* a *very* interesting book *Presently* we will read the book.
6. Prepositions	Used before nouns and pronouns to relate them to other words in the sentence	*to* the house *with* extra food for them
7. Conjunctions	Connect words, phrases, or clauses; may be coordinators or subordinators	prose *and* poetry before *or* after *since* Tuesday
8. Interjections	Expressions of emotion unrelated to the rest of the sentence	Wow! He's finished!

1d A phrase is a group of words that functions as a single part of speech.

Phrases do not have subjects or predicates and function as single parts of speech. A phrase may function as a noun, a verb, an adjective, or an adverb, depending upon how it is used in a sentence. For example, a noun phrase could function as a subject, an object, or a complement. A phrase that modifies a noun or pronoun would be an adjective phrase. Gerund, participial, and infinitive phrases perform the same functions as described in the section on verbals in 1b.

EXAMPLES:

Verb phrase:	John *could have gone* home.
Noun phrase:	*The unprepared student* was sent home.
Prepositional phrase:	Marcia went *to her room.*

Verbal phrases

Gerund phrase:	*Arguing with him* does little good.
Participial phrase:	*Having given him the required work*, I left.
Infinitive phrase:	We stood up *to see better.*

1e Recognizing clauses helps in analyzing sentences.

A clause is a group of related words that contains a subject and a predicate. There are two types of clauses: *independent* clauses and *subordinate* (or *dependent*) clauses.

> *Independent clauses* have subjects and predicates, and are actually sentences. The definition can be reversed: sentences are independent clauses.
>
> > Jean went to school.
>
> *Subordinate clauses* are groups of related words that contain subjects and predicates, but cannot stand alone. They have subordinators—words that qualify the meaning of the clause and require that they be attached to independent clauses.
>
> > Jean went to school *although* she wasn't feeling well.

Subordinate clauses function within a sentence as a single part of speech and are linked to an independent clause by a *subordinating conjunction* (*although, because, if,* etc.) or a *relative pronoun* (*who, which, that,* etc.).

Noun clause:	*What you were told about the books* is true. [subject]

Adjective clause: We need information *that is accurate*. [modifies *information*]
Adverbial clause: He sent the application *after the college asked for it*.
                    [modifies *sent*]

COMMONLY USED SUBORDINATORS

after	if	until
although	in order that	when
as	since	whenever
as if	so that	where
as though	that	wherever
because	though	while
before	unless	who

RELATIVE PRONOUNS

that	who	whomever
what	whoever	whose
which	whom	

1f   Sentences may be analyzed by form and function. The form is identified by the number and kinds of clauses it contains, and the function of a sentence refers to its purpose.

There are four possible forms a sentence may take.

1. *Simple* sentence—consists of a single independent clause.

   Margo will graduate from high school.

2. *Compound* sentence—consists of at least two independent clauses.

   Margo will graduate from high school, and she will go to college.

3. *Complex* sentence—consists of one independent clause and at least one subordinate clause.

   Even though her grades were good, she was required to take a placement test.

4. *Compound/complex* sentence—consists of at least two independent clauses and at least one subordinate clause.

   Once she passed the test, she was admitted to the college of her choice, but she later chose a different college because it was closer to home.

There are four functions of sentences.

1. *Declarative*—makes a statement.

   She passed the test.

2. *Imperative*—makes a request or gives a command.

   Take that test now.

3. *Interrogative*—asks a question.

   Did you take the test?

4. *Exclamatory*—makes an exclamation.

   What a test! She passed it!

Basic Sentence Parts—Verbs   Exercise 1–1

NAME _____ SCORE _____

DIRECTIONS: In the following paragraph, underline the subject of each sentence with one line, the predicate with two lines, and the complement, if there is one, with three lines.

EXAMPLE

The teacher gave an assignment to the class. John finished before the rest of the class.

[1]When Marcia was a senior in high school, she was a member of the debating team. [2]She also worked after school in a supermarket. [3]Extra time was scarce. [4]She had to stay up late to study. [5]She slept soundly and woke up early. [6]Marcia ate breakfast on the run and studied her assignments on the school bus. [7]She plans to rest this summer, even though she will work. [8]Next fall she starts college.

Which verbs have prepositions? List them.

_____

_____

_____

_____

_____

_____

Which verbs have auxiliaries? List them.

_____

_____

_____

_____

_____

_____

Basic Sentence Parts—Subjects

Exercise 1–2

NAME _____ SCORE _____

DIRECTIONS: Read the following paragraph. In each of the sentences, underline the subject(s) with one line, and the predicate with two lines. Beneath the paragraph, indicate whether the subject of that sentence is a noun (n) or pronoun (p), and whether it is a single (s) or compound (c) subject.

EXAMPLE

[1]John and Marie played sports in high school. [2]They enjoyed what they did.

1. n, n, c
2. p, s

[1]Marie and Mark will graduate this year. [2]Both of them are going to college. [3]They are preparing now for next September. [4]Let them be an example for you. [5]Don't wait until the last minute to plan your academic year. [6]Marie plans to major in nursing. [7]Mark wants to be an engineer.

1. _____
2. _____
3. _____
4. _____
5. _____
6. _____
7. _____

Basic Sentence Parts—Complements   Exercise 1–3

NAME _____   SCORE _____

DIRECTIONS: Read the following paragraph. Underline the subject with one line, the predicate with two lines, and the complement with three lines. Beneath the paragraph there are numbers corresponding to the numbers of the sentences. Next to the number, write each complement that appears in that sentence and indicate whether it is a direct object (do), indirect object (io), subject complement (sc), or object complement (oc).

EXAMPLE

    1. The school gave Marie an award.

    2. She was thrilled.

    3. She made her parents proud.

        1. Marie (io); award (do)
        2. thrilled (sc)
        3. parents (do); proud (oc)

    [1]Marcia and John will go to college next September. [2]They have already bought their books. [3]Actually, Marcia became the book-buyer. [4]She bought John's and her own books. [5]They both seem anxious to leave home. [6]The college gave them each a reading list for the summer. [7]John's list was longer than Marcia's because the Engineering Department requires more literature and history than the Nursing Department. [8]The list Marcia received, however, seems more difficult because of the anatomy and physiology books she will have to study.

1. _____

2. _____

3. _____

4. _____

5. _____

6. _____

7. _____

8. _____

Parts of Speech   Exercise 1–4

NAME _____ SCORE _____

DIRECTIONS: Write a sentence for each of the eight parts of speech. Underline the function you have chosen in each sentence.

EXAMPLES

   1. Verbs   John <u>would have liked</u> the party.
   2. Nouns   <u>Marie</u> and <u>Ed</u> went to the <u>store</u>.

1. Verbs   _____

2. Nouns   _____

3. Pronouns _____

4. Adjectives _____

5. Adverbs   _____

6. Prepositions _____

7. Conjunctions _____

8. Interjections _____

Verbals   Exercise 1–5

NAME _____   SCORE _____

DIRECTIONS: Write a sentence for each of the three types of verbals. Underline the verbal, and indicate its function in the sentence.

EXAMPLE

Gerund	He enjoys <u>jogging</u>.
Function	object of the verb

1. Gerund   _____

   _____

   Function   _____

2. Participle _____

   _____

   Function   _____

3. Infinitive _____

   _____

   Function   _____

Phrases

Exercise 1–6

NAME _____ SCORE _____

DIRECTIONS: Underline the phrases in the following paragraph. List the phrases in each sentence, and indicate the type of phrase it is.

EXAMPLE

Arguing with him won't get him to change his mind.

Arguing with him; gerund phrase
to change his mind; prepositional phrase

[1]At their high school graduation ceremony, Marcia and Edward went dressed formally. [2]After the ceremony, a group of their friends, to make them happy, invited them to a party at Maria's house. [3]Edward's father, concerned about their driving carefully, took them in his car to make sure they arrived safely. [4]At 1:00 a.m., he went back to pick them up.

1. _____

_____

_____

2. _____

_____

_____

3. _____

_____

_____

4. _____

_____

_____

Clauses   Exercise 1–7

NAME _____ SCORE _____

DIRECTIONS: Reorganize and rewrite the following paragraph, combining sentences and converting as many independent clauses as you can into subordinate
clauses without changing the sense and meaning of the paragraph. Above each
subordinate clause you write indicate whether it is a noun (n) clause, an adjective (adj) clause, or an adverbial (adv) clause.

EXAMPLE

[1]Sam went to the store. [2]He went to shop. [3]Sam drove his father's car.
[4]He had a lot to buy.

Sam went to the store so he could shop. Since he had a lot to buy, he drove his
father's car.

[1]John and Maria finished high school. [2]They graduated in June. [3]They will go to college. [4]Next fall they start. [5]John will major in humanities. [6]He wants to be a teacher.
[7]Maria wants to be a doctor. [8]She will major in biology. [9]They are going to a state
college. [10]They are both going to the same state college. [11]They leave home in September. [12]They have never lived away from home before. [13]John and Maria are
excited about going to college. [14]They can't wait until September. [15]Their parents
will drive them. [16]It's an important part of their lives.

_____

_____

_____

_____

_____

_____

_____

_____

_____

Sentence Forms and Functions

Exercise 1–8

NAME _____ SCORE _____

DIRECTIONS: For each of the following sentences, indicate in the first blank whether the sentence is simple, compound, complex, or compound/complex. In the second blank, indicate whether the sentence is declarative, imperative, interrogative, or exclamatory.

EXAMPLE

    1. Take this home and fix it. _compound_ _imperative_

    2. Isn't that correct? _simple_ _interrogative_

1. Go. _____ _____

2. Is that correct, even though you've been taught differently?

    _____ _____

3. Studying for exams isn't easy, but the consequences of not studying should make you want to study.

    _____ _____

4. The senior year of high school is an important transition in a person's life.

    _____ _____

5. Life is easier when you're well prepared.

    _____ _____

6. Freshman year in college can be very rewarding if you are mentally prepared for it.

    _____ _____

7. The first year of college is socially active, but don't forget your academic obligations.

    _____ _____

8. Whatever you do, don't get involved with students whose only concern is partying.

    _____ _____

9. Getting poor grades in your first year stays with you throughout college; you're always trying to make up for early mistakes.

   _____   _____

10. Good grades in the first year of college provide a base for a high average when you graduate; look to the future.

   _____   _____

Chapter 2

Sentence Fragments

(Hodges 2)   frag 1

A fragment is a group of words that is used to communicate a thought but is missing either a subject, a verb, or both, and therefore cannot be considered to be a sentence. Phrases and subordinate clauses are frequently used to communicate in conversation, but when we write in English, this type of communication is normally considered grammatically incorrect.

2a   Phrases are sometimes mistakenly punctuated as sentences.

If you use a verbal instead of a verb, you create a fragment.

Verbal Phrase	The importance of graduating from high school *having been* the topic.
Sentence	The importance of graduating from high school *was* the topic.

A prepositional phrase should not be punctuated as a sentence.

Prepositional phrase	From the beginning of his speech.
Sentence	He held our attention from the beginning of his speech to the end.

COMMONLY USED PREPOSITIONS

across	for	over
after	from	through
as	in	to
at	in front of	under
because of	in regard to	until
before	like	up
beside	near	with
between	of	
by	on	

An appositive is a word or group of words that follows a noun or pronoun and explains, defines, or restates the noun or pronoun. An appositive cannot stand alone as a sentence and is considered a fragment if punctuated as a sentence.

Appositive	A great civil rights leader.
Sentence	Rev. Martin Luther King, a great civil rights leader, was assassinated in 1968.

By separating two parts of a compound predicate you can create a fragment.

Predicate	And bought all her books.
Sentence	Maria went to the bookstore and bought all her books.

2b   Subordinate clauses are sometimes mistakenly punctuated as sentences.

Whenever you place a subordinate before or after the subject, you create a fragment. Remove the subordinator or attach the fragment to an appropriate sentence.

Subordinate clause	Jackie Robinson *who* was the first African-American to play major league baseball.
Sentence	Jackie Robinson was the first African-American to play major league baseball.
Subordinate clause	Jackie Robinson played second base for the Dodgers. Who used to play at Ebbett's Field in Brooklyn.
Sentence	Jackie Robinson played second base for the Dodgers, who used to play at Ebbett's Field in Brooklyn.

Summary

Since a fragment is missing an element that would make it a sentence, it is important to determine what that element is. First, make sure your sentences have verbs (*not* verbals) by asking yourself, "Where or what or how is the action in this sentence?" Once you determine that, ask yourself, "Who or what is performing the action?" You will determine, first, whether you have a subject, and second, who or what the subject is. If you are missing the verb, a subject, or both, you have written a fragment and can correct it either by supplying the missing part or parts it needs to make it a sentence or by connecting the fragment to a sentence to which it is related. When you have a subordinate clause written as a sentence, remove the subordinator or attach the clause to a related sentence.

Phrases Used as Fragments

Exercise 2–1

NAME _____ SCORE _____

DIRECTIONS: For each of the following fragments, indicate in the first column whether it is a verbal phrase (v), prepositional phrase (p), appositive (a), or separated compound predicate (sp). In the second column, indicate whether that fragment is missing a subject (subj), verb (verb), or both (subj/verb).

EXAMPLE

With each of the books.	p	subj/verb
John going to dinner.	v	verb

1. Having been there myself _____ _____

2. One of the best second-basemen who ever played _____ _____

3. With the best of them _____ _____

4. Stealing bases a specialty _____ _____

5. To everyone who saw him _____ _____

6. And gave the speech on time _____ _____

7. During a philosophy class Monday _____ _____

8. John reading from his notes _____ _____

9. Who is well known in his field _____ _____

10. His hitting as well as his fielding _____ _____

11. John studying the history of baseball _____ _____

12. His surprise at finding the Dodgers had played in Brooklyn _____ _____

13. The home of many legends about baseball _____ _____

14. Before college John knowing nothing about it _____ _____

15. And learned about it now _____ _____

Subordinate Clauses Used as Fragments   Exercise 2–2

NAME _____   SCORE _____

DIRECTIONS: Rewrite the following subordinate clauses, and make them correct sentences. You may add independent clauses where necessary.

EXAMPLE

Fragment	Mark went to the library. Where he studied.
Sentence	Mark went to the library, where he studied.
	or Mark went to the library to study.
Fragment	The library which is where Mark can study.
Sentence	The library is a place where Mark can study.

1. Because it was late at night.

_____

_____

2. He left the lecture before it was finished. Although the professor was upset.

_____

_____

3. John studied all night. Even though he was tired.

_____

_____

4. Until you get better grades.

_____

_____

5. However, Marie's grades which were better than John's.

_____

_____

6. John and Marie wanted to do well on the College Placement Test. Which was scheduled for Saturday.

_____

_____

7. Between studying and working, little free time for socializing.

   _____

   _____

8. They didn't understand the assignment. Because of being absent.

   _____

   _____

9. In regard to Friday's English test.

   _____

   _____

10. As for the exam, John and Marie passed. Because of studying together.

    _____

    _____

Chapter 3

Comma Splices and Fused Sentences

(*Hodges* 3)   cs/fs 1

Splicing and fusing are two processes that join items such as broken or melted wires or broken pieces of wood. These items are put back together and mended, but are never again as strong or sturdy as they once had been. When these terms are used in reference to sentences, the same principle applies; two independent clauses are joined with binding (the comma) that is too weak to keep the parts (clauses) together, or they are joined with no binding at all (fused).

Comma splice	Many students hold part-time jobs while attending college, work shouldn't take priority over studying.
Fused sentence	Many students hold part-time jobs while attending college work shouldn't take priority over studying.

Comma splices and fused sentences can usually be corrected by using the same remedies for both. For example, a period can always be used to make two complete sentences out of the two independent clauses that are spliced or fused. Another method of correcting a comma splice or fused sentence is to subordinate one of the clauses. (See also *Harbrace* 9; *Hodges* 24.)

Two sentences	Many students hold part-time jobs while attending college. Work shouldn't take priority over studying.
Subordination	Although many students hold part-time jobs while attending college, work shouldn't take priority over studying.

3a   Commas occur between independent clauses only when they are linked by a coordinating conjunction (*and, but, or, for, not, so, yet*). (See also *Harbrace* 18a; *Hodges* 14a.)

Many students hold part-time jobs while attending college, *but* work shouldn't take priority over studying.

3b   Semicolons occur before conjunctive adverbs or transitional phrases that are placed between independent clauses. (See also *Harbrace* 18a, *Hodges* 14a.)

Conjunctive adverb   Many students hold part-time jobs while attending college; *however*, work shouldn't take priority over studying.

Transitional phrase   Many students hold part-time jobs while attending college; *on the other hand*, work shouldn't take priority over studying.

CONJUNCTIVE ADVERBS

accordingly	henceforth	nevertherless
also	however	nonetheless
anyhow	indeed	otherwise
besides	instead	similarly
consequently	likewise	still
finally	meanwhile	then
first, second, etc.	moreover	therefore
furthermore	next	thus
hence		

COMMONLY USED TRANSITIONAL PHRASES

after all	even so	in other words
as a result	for example	in the second place
at any rate	for instance	on the contrary
at the same time	in addition	on the other hand
by the way	in fact	that is

3c   Divided quotations can trick you into making a comma splice. (See also *Harbrace* 20, *Hodges* 16f.)

Comma splice   "Where are my books?" John asked, "I can't find them."
Revised   "Where are my books?" John asked. "I can't find them."

Comma Splices and Fused Sentences   Exercise 3–1

NAME _____ SCORE _____

DIRECTIONS: For each of the following sentences, indicate in the first blank whether the sentence is correct according to standard practice (c), contains a comma splice (cs), or is fused (f). In the second blank, indicate whether you would correct the sentence, if necessary, by (A) making two complete sentences, (B) using a semicolon with conjunctive adverb, (C) using a semicolon with transitional phrase, or (D) using a semicolon alone.

EXAMPLE

I want to major in medicine I want to help   <u>f</u>   <u>B or D</u>
the less fortunate.

1. The first semester of college is the most difficult,   _____   _____
   there are many distractions.

2. It takes practice to make a good schedule I had too   _____   _____
   much time between classes my first semester in college.

3. I had never been away from home before, I missed my   _____   _____
   familiar surroundings.

4. Jobs are available on campus, there's a placement   _____   _____
   office to help students who are looking for work.

5. You have to learn your way around the library term   _____   _____
   papers require research.

6. There are many ways to learn, taking courses in   _____   _____
   specialized areas is one life experience is another.

7. We learn about life by meeting people from different   _____   _____
   backgrounds and finding out how they live.

8. I fell asleep in class last week as a result I had to   _____   _____
   reduce the number of hours I work after school.

9. I made friends with someone from South America,   _____   _____
   I met the person in the cafeteria while having lunch
   in addition we're in the same math class, so I get
   help with my Spanish homework.

10. My English professor told me that my writing   _____   _____
    contained good ideas however, I had to improve
    my sentence structure.

Comma Splices and Fused Sentences   Exercise 3–2

NAME _____ SCORE _____

DIRECTIONS: In the space provided, indicate whether the sentence is fused or contains a comma splice. Then rewrite each sentence eliminating comma splices and correcting fused sentences.

1. I needed help revising my conclusion, my peer tutor helped me refocus it.

   _____

   _____

   _____

   _____

2. The library contains several manuals for using computer programs, likewise, the librarians offer workshops to teach students how to use certain computer programs.

   _____

   _____

   _____

   _____

3. I suddenly remembered that my class would meet in the library, I quickly picked up my books and left the classroom.

   _____

   _____

   _____

   _____

4. I can't study with the television on it distracts me.

   _____

   _____

   _____

   _____

5. We had two hours to finish the test I finished in one hour.

6. The professor divided the class into small groups, each group was assigned an issue to discuss.

7. My roommate eats her lunch in our dormitory room, I usually eat in the cafeteria with friends.

8. Painting is one of my favorite hobbies it is very relaxing.

9. His friends went to the football game, however he couldn't go with them because he had to study.

10. Biology is your first class today isn't it?

Harcourt Brace & Company

Review: Comma Splices, Fused Sentences, Fragments

NAME _____ SCORE _____

DIRECTIONS: Rewrite the following paragraph, correcting any comma splices, fused sentences, or sentence fragments.

   [1]Now that you have become accustomed to writing grammatically correct sentences. [2]It shouldn't be difficult to develop good paragraphs they come naturally once sentence structure is mastered. [3]Ideas flow, you can put them down on paper easily and writing sentences correctly becomes second nature. [4]Being good at this. [5]It's easy and gets easier with practice. [6]So practice good, correct writing in all of your courses. [7]Not just your English classes. [8]You'll appreciate the ability to write well later when you apply for a job. [9]After you graduate. [10]Time flies, and that day will come before you know it.

_____

_____

_____

_____

_____

_____

_____

_____

_____

_____

_____

_____

_____

_____

_____

_____

_____

_____

Chapter 4

Adjectives and Adverbs

(Hodges 4)   ad 4

Adjectives and adverbs are words that modify other words. Modify means they affect the meanings of other words by changing or qualifying those meanings so that the modified words are more clear. Adjectives modify nouns or pronouns; adverbs modify verbs, adjectives, or other adverbs. Both adjectives and adverbs may be used in the same sentence.

> Marie and Marcia *quickly* carried the *heavy* textbooks to their *crowded* dormitory.

The adverb *quickly* modifies the verb *carried*. It tells you how the books were carried. The adjective *heavy* modifies the noun *textbooks*. It tells you something about the textbooks. The adjective *crowded* modifies the noun *dormitory*. It tells you the condition of the dormitory.

Adverbs can also modify verbals and whole clauses. An entire clause could function as an adverb or an adjective.

> *Paying attention regularly* is important. [Adverb *regularly* modifies the verbal *paying*, which is a gerund functioning as the subject.]

> *When he went to his dormitory,* he found visitors. [An adverbial clause of time that modifies the verb *found*.]

> John found visitors *who were sitting in his room.* [An adverbial clause that modifies the object *visitors*.]

4a   Adverbs modify verbs, adjectives, and other adverbs.

When an adverb modifies a verb, it is telling you how, when, or where the action occurred.

> Marie studied the lesson *completely*. [*Completely* is an adverb that modifies the verb *studied*; it tells you how the lesson was studied.]

The test took a *fairly* long time. [*Fairly* is an adverb that modifies the adjective *long*; it tells you how long the test took.]

4b There is a distinction between adverbs used to modify verbs and adjectives used as subject or object complements.

John felt *weary*. [subject complement]

John continued *wearily*. [adverb]

Marie found John *tired*. [*Tired* is an adjective that refers to the direct object *John* and completes the meaning of the verb *found*.]

4c Many adjectives and adverbs change form to indicate the degree of comparison.

The comparison degree is used for comparing two, and the superlative degree is used for three or more. The comparative is usually formed by adding "er" to the modifier or by putting *more* or *less* before the modifier. The superlative is usually formed by adding "est" to the modifier or by putting *most* or *least* before the modifier.

Light, lighter, lightest
Dark, darker, darkest
Slowly, more slowly, most slowly

Some modifiers are irregular in form.

Good, better, best
Bad, worse, worst

Modifiers that end in "y" change the "y" to "i" when changing to comparative or superlative.

Happy, happier, happiest
Lucky, luckier, luckiest

It is incorrect to use a double comparative or superlative.

More luckier, most happiest

4d   Use of a word group or a noun as an adjective can be awkward or ambiguous.

Occasionally, it is correct to use nouns as modifiers of other nouns, but when adjectives are available avoid the awkward use of nouns.

Awkward   Teacher faculty require different training than administrator faculty.

Better   Teaching faculty require different training than administrative faculty.

4e   A single rather than a double negative is correct.

The double negative, like the double comparison, is incorrect.

I didn't not need that.

He couldn't hardly get there in time.

Adjectives and Adverbs   Exercise 4–1

NAME _____   SCORE _____

DIRECTIONS: For each of the following sentences, write in the space provided the correct form of the modifier that appears in parentheses. Indicate next to your answer whether it is an adjective (adj) or an adverb (adv). You should consult your dictionary whenever necessary.

EXAMPLE

His car is (new) than her car.   _newer, adj._

He did his homework (quick).   _quickly, adv._

1. The organization of Martha's term paper was (perfect).

   _____

2. The professor said it was done (perfect) as well as (neat).

   _____

3. It was one of the (good) projects she had ever done.

   _____

4. The good grade she received made her (happy) than she had ever been.

   _____

5. Now it was John's turn to see if he could write (good) than she.

   _____

6. Planning (careful) is an important step when writing.

   _____

7. John (certain) is (careful).

   _____

8. He found the project (tired), and was (happy) when it was finished.

   _____

9. His grade was (high) than Martha's.

   _____

10. The (literature) society gave them both awards for (hardly not) making mistakes.

   _____

Harcourt Brace & Company   **43**

11. Next semester they will take an advanced writing course which is (difficult).

_____

12. It is a good idea to write (quick) on an exam so you have enough time to finish.

_____

13. There's (not no) opportunity to make up for lost time.

_____

14. Some students end up (desperate) trying to finish an exam.

_____

15. You would be (lucky) to pass if you waste time, and (happy) if you're (careful) to budget your time.

_____

Adjectives and Adverbs   Exercise 4–2

NAME _____ SCORE _____

DIRECTIONS: After each of the following adjectives, write the comparative form in the first column and the superlative form in the second column. In the third column, convert the original adjective into an adverb.

EXAMPLE

warm   <u>warmer</u>   <u>warmest</u>   <u>warmly</u>

1. new   _____   _____   _____

2. swift   _____   _____   _____

3. little   _____   _____   _____

4. bad   _____   _____   _____

5. slow   _____   _____   _____

6. happy   _____   _____   _____

7. ill   _____   _____   _____

8. fortunate _____   _____   _____

9. good   _____   _____   _____

10. friendly _____   _____   _____

Chapter 5

Coherence: Misplaced Parts and Dangling Modifiers

(*Hodges* 25)   mp/dm 5

In English, it is important to maintain coherence in sentences, paragraphs, and throughout an essay. On the level of the sentence, coherence means all parts of the sentence are consistent and logically integrated. Always keep modifiers as near as possible to the words they modify; the position of the modifier could change the meaning of the sentence.

5a   Placing modifiers near the words they modify clarifies meaning.

John *just* went to the bookstore.
John went *just* to the bookstore.

He was *almost* late for class.

He *nearly* missed the lecture.

Prepositional phrases should be placed so that it is clear what they modify.

Unclear	Marie wanted *in the morning* to go to class.
Clear	Marie wanted to go to class *in the morning*.

Adjective clauses should be placed near the words they modify.

Unclear	I bought the books from the bookstore that I needed for English.
Clear	I bought the books that I needed from the bookstore.

Use good judgment when splitting an infinitive.

Awkward	John quickly drove fast to get there.
Unclear	John drove fast quickly to get there.
Clear	John drove fast to quickly get there.

5b   There are several ways to revise dangling modifiers.

A dangling modifier doesn't clearly refer to other words or phrases in the sentence. It can be any word, phrase, or clause that is misplaced.

Dangling	The weekend passed quickly, studying and talking.
Revised	The weekend passed quickly because we were studying and talking.
Dangling	Going to the game, it was cold in November.
Revised	It can be cold going to the game in November.
Dangling	Walking down the street, the house was to our left.
Revised	Walking down the street, we saw the house on our left.

Placement of Modifiers   Exercise 5–1

NAME _____ SCORE _____

DIRECTIONS: Rearrange and rewrite the following sentences, placing any misplaced modifiers as near as possible to the word or words they modify. In the
space provided, write the word or words being modified. If a sentence is correctly written, write C in the space provided.

EXAMPLE

Marie only wore her coat, and everyone else was cold.   <u>Marie</u>

<u>   Only Marie wore her coat, and everyone else was cold.   </u>

1. John finished almost his lunch.   _____

   _____

2. Marie was even late for class.   _____

   _____

3. Ed went the next day to class.   _____

   _____

4. He took the books to the classroom that he had just   _____
   bought.

   _____

5. Marie wrote a letter at her desk about her schedule.   _____

   _____

6. The letter was written when she was upset to her   _____
   mother.

   _____

7. They all agreed nearly that college was not like high   _____
   school.

   _____

8. They wanted to just improve their study habits.   _____

   _____

9. The test would be difficult that they would take on Monday.   _____

10. It would be an important grade for almost all of them.   _____

Dangling Modifiers   Exercise 5–2

NAME _____   SCORE _____

DIRECTIONS: Rearrange and rewrite the following sentences, eliminating any dangling modifiers. You may add or change words to make the meanings clear.

EXAMPLE

The man was caught by the police looking in the window.

   The police caught the man who was looking in the window.

1. Remembered by her mother, dinner was delayed because Marie was still at school.

   _____

   _____

2. Their grades could have been better, but they hadn't studied enough playing football on Sunday.

   _____

   _____

3. Walking to the parking lot the car was at the far end so it took a while to find it.

   _____

   _____

4. While in high school, my father took me to the library every Saturday.

   _____

   _____

5. To get good grades, good notes are needed to study.

   _____

   _____

Chapter 6

Pronouns

(*Hodges* 5, 6b, 28)

Pronouns perform several different functions in sentences. They can be subjects or objects, and they can be used to show possession or ownership. Pronouns have a variety of forms that show their relationship to other parts of the sentence. These forms are known as *cases*, and there are three cases: subjective, possessive, and objective.

> He [the subject] went to my [modifier showing possession] car to get a book for me [object of the preposition].

In addition to case, pronouns have singular and plural forms.

> I [singular] want us [plural] to get our [plural] gift for her [singular].

	SINGULAR	PLURAL
Subjective	I	we
	you	you
	he, she, it	they
Possessive	my, mine	our, ours
	your, yours	your, yours
	his, her, its	their, theirs
Objective	me	us
	you	you
	him, her, it	them

There are three types of pronouns: *personal, intensive/reflexive,* and *relative.*

The **personal pronouns** identify the speaker [first person: *I, we*], the person spoken to [second person: *you*], and the person or thing spoken about [third person: *he, she, it, they*]. The pronouns *I, we, he, she,* and *they* have distinctive forms for all three cases and for both singular and plural. *You* is the same in both singular and plural, and *you* and *it* change case forms only in the possessive, becoming *your* and *its*.

The **intensive/reflexive pronouns** *my, our, your, him, her, it,* and *them* combine with *self* or *selves* for emphasis. Intensive/reflexive pronouns often refer to a noun or pronoun already mentioned in the sentence, and always follow the person or thing to which they refer.

> *Intensive*   Marie, *herself*, drove the car.
>
> *Reflexive*   They all saw the picture of *themselves*

Relative pronouns [*who, whom, whose,* and *that*] introduce clauses that refer to a noun in the main clause.

> Marcia, *who* wrote the paper, had to rewrite it.

Who, whose, and *whom* usually refer to people; *which* to things; and *that* to either. The possessive pronoun *whose*, in place of *of which*, sometimes refers to things.

> The dog, *whose* owner is away, barked all night.

6a   Pronouns agree with their antecedents.

The subject of a verb and the subject complement are in the subjective case.

> *It* was *I* who drove her there.

The object of a verb, verbal, or preposition is in the objective case.

> John called *me*. [direct object]
>
> Driving *her* is a task. [indirect object]
>
> He gave *them* his keys. [indirect object]
>
> With *whom* were you talking? [object of preposition]

Pronouns should agree in number and gender with the noun or phrase (antecedent) to which they refer.

> John gave *his* speech.
>
> Marie gave *her* speech.
>
> They gave *their* speeches.

When you need to refer to a noun that can be either male or female, there are four ways to avoid using *he*.

Drop the pronoun entirely.

A student should communicate with parents.

Change the entire sentence to the plural.

Students should communicate with their parents.

Use the passive voice.

Parents should be communicated with by students.

Use the imperative.

Students—communicate with your parents.

6b   Pronouns refer to the nouns immediately preceding them.

Avoid inserting any word, words, or phrases between a noun (antecedent) and a reference pronoun since this could confuse the reader. Be certain the antecedent is clearly recognizable.

Unclear	John gave Ed *his* keys.
Clear	John gave *his* keys to Ed.
Remote	The class was held in a large lecture hall, *which* was difficult and lengthy.
Better	The class, *which* was difficult and lengthy, was held in a large lecture hall.

6c   Pronoun form in compound constructions varies.

Multiple subjects or subject complements are in the subjective case.

He and *she* went to school together.

It was *she* and *I* who rewrote the paper.

Multiple objects of prepositions are in the objective case.

John went with *her* and *me*.

Multiple objects of verbs or verbals and subjects of infinitives are in the objective case.

The professor might call *you* or *me*. [direct object]

He gave *John* and *her* the assignment. [indirect object]

Bothering *him* and *her* won't accomplish anything. [object of gerund]

The professor told *Marcia* and *me* to speak. [subject of infinitive]

6d   The use of a pronoun in its own clause determines its case.

I know *who* wrote the paper. [*Who* is subject of the dependent clause *who wrote the paper.*]

Help is available for *whoever* wants it. [*Whoever* is subject of the clause *whoever wants it*; The clause is object of the preposition *for*.]

Use *whom* as an object in formal written English.

Better grades were earned by the students *whom* they had helped. [*Whom* is object of the verb *helped*.]

The choice of pronoun form can influence meaning in sentences where something is implied.

Marie studies more than *I*. [subjective case, meaning "spends more time studying than I do"]

Marie studies more than *me*. [objective case, meaning "studies more lessons than me"]

6e   A pronoun before a gerund uses the possessive form.

John helped Marie, and the professor rewarded *his* helping her.

6f   Pronouns use the objective form for the subject or the object of an infinitive.

They asked *her* to help *him*.

6g   Pronouns use the subjective form for a subject complement.

It was *I* who helped her.

Reference of Pronouns   Exercise 6–1

NAME _____ SCORE _____

DIRECTIONS: For each of the following sentences, choose the correct pronoun form (case) wherever there is a blank. Write the correct pronoun in the space provided.

EXAMPLE

When my parents let me use their car, they insist I pay for my
own fuel before giving it back to _____.   _them_

1. That car is _____.   _____

2. They got tired of _____ talking about it.   _____

3. Talk it over with _____ and see how   _____

    _____ feel about the issues.   _____

4. _____ going into the Armed Forces before college   _____

    is a possibility.

5. She and _____ discussed the subject at length.   _____

6. John convinced _____ he was making the right decision. _____

7. His parents didn't want any more of _____ vacillating. _____

8. "Your mother and _____ want you to decide,"   _____

    his father said to _____.   _____

9. John, _____started the discussion, wanted to end it. _____

10. Between you and _____, Marie should help John decide. _____

11. I, _____, told him to go to college first.   _____

12. The ultimate winner is _____.   _____

13. The people to _____ he gave an answer are   _____

    his closest friends.

14. The professor _____ they are corresponding with was _____

    happy someone, _____ it might be, made a decision.   _____

15. It doesn't matter _____ decision it is.   _____

Agreement of Pronouns and Antecedents   Exercise 6–2

NAME _____ SCORE _____

DIRECTIONS: In each of the following sentences, underline the subject of the sentence with one line; cross out the incorrect reference pronoun in the parentheses, and rewrite the correct one in the space provided.

EXAMPLE

John went to the bookstore to get (his, ~~her~~) supplies.   __his__

1. John gave (I, me) the book.   _____

2. It was (I, me) who bought the tickets.   _____

3. John, (who, whom) arrived late, missed the show.   _____

4. The campus was renovated and had (their, its)   _____

   windows cleaned.

5. A teacher should respect (his, her, their) students.   _____

6. Everybody should keep (his, her, their) room clean.   _____

7. Telling (they, them) is important.   _____

8. The students gave (his, her, their) views on the subject.   _____

9. Don't blame (I, me) for failing the test.   _____

10. Marie told (I, me) the news.   _____

Chapter 7

Verbs

(Hodges 7, 6a) v 7

Verbs express action, existence, or occurrence. Verbs in English show what the subject is doing or being, when the action occurred or will occur, and as you will see in this chapter, they function as the main part of a sentence. In fact, you cannot have a sentence without a verb. Verbs are complicated, but you must become knowledgeable about them in order to become proficient in written as well as spoken English.

There are several aspects to verbs.

Tense   The tense of a verb shows the time of an action—present, past, future. The action could have begun in the past and ended, or it could be continuing through the present and into the future. All this is reflected in the form of a verb. There are six tenses in English. Three are called simple, and three are called perfect. Perfect tenses refer to the time in which the action began and the time in which the action is completed.

SIMPLE TENSES

Present: We study our lessons.
Past: We studied our lessons.
Future: We will study our lessons.

PERFECT TENSES

Present: We have studied our lessons.
Past: We had studied our lessons.
Future: We will have studied our lessons.

Regular and irregular verbs   Regular verbs denote the past tense by using a *-d* or *-ed* ending. Irregular verbs form the past tense differently.

Regular   talk (talks), talked

Irregular   bring (brings), brought

Harcourt Brace & Company   **61**

Auxiliary verbs   Also called helping verbs, auxiliary verbs combine with main verbs to indicate tense, voice, or mood. Consult your dictionary for correct information on usage. (See also *Harbrace* 13, *Hodges* 19.)

AUXILIARY VERBS		MODAL AUXILIARY VERBS (COMBINE WITH PRESENT TENSE)	
be	have	shall	may
am	has	should	might
is	had	will	must
are	do	would	can
was	does		could
were	did		
being	been		

Forms of **be**   The verb *to be* is the most irregular verb in English, and the easiest to misuse. Be sure to use the correct form when speaking and writing. The forms of the verb *to be* are:

PRESENT	I am, we are	you are	he/she/it is, they are
PAST	I was, we were	you were	he/she/it was, they were
FUTURE	I/we will *or* shall be	you will *or* shall be	he/she/it they will *or* shall be
PAST/PRESENT PERFECT	I/we have been	you have been	he/she/it has been, they have been
FUTURE PERFECT	am are had been has been	have been is was were	will *or* shall be will *or* shall have been

Voice   The **voice** of a verb shows the relationship between the action of the verb and the subject. In English, there are two possible voices: the **active voice**, where the subject is doing the action, and the **passive voice**, where the action is being done to the subject.

Active   Marie *studies* her lessons.
Passive   The lessons *are studied* by Marie.

Transitive and intransitive verbs Transitive verbs are able to accept direct objects. **Intransitive verbs** cannot accept direct objects but can take subject complements. Consult your dictionary to find out whether a verb is transitive, intransitive, or both.

Transitive   John *drove* the car. [*car*, the direct object, receives the action of *drove*]

Intransitive   The answer *appears* correct. [*correct* is the subject complement, identifying *answer*]

Mood The **mood** of a verb shows the attitude of the speaker or writer. There are three moods in English: the **indicative mood**, which makes statements and conveys a definite attitude; the **imperative mood**, which issues commands or requests and conveys an insistent attitude; and the **subjunctive mood**, which expresses the conditional or hypothetical and conveys a tentative attitude.

Indicative   You are studying.

Imperative   Study.

Subjunctive   If you would study, it might help.

7a Verbs must agree with their subjects.

Subject and verb must match in number.

John studies alone.

Neither the books nor the cover was available. [Note: with a compound subject, the verb agrees with the nearer subject.]

John or Marie studies.

John and Marie study.

Some indefinite pronouns, such as *each, either, one, everybody*, and *anyone*, are singular and take singular verbs. Other indefinite pronouns, such as *all, any, some, none, half*, and *most*, can be either singular or plural, depending on the sentence.

Anyone who has succeeded in college *has* studied.

He read all those books, and *some were* good.

He checked the ice cream, and *some was* melted.

Collective nouns and phrases can take a singular or plural verb, depending on the meaning or sense of the sentence. If the sentence refers to the group as a whole, the verb is singular. If the sentence refers to individual items, the verb is plural.

The football *team is* playing today.
Football team *members are* playing today.

Five thousand *spectators fills* the stadium.
Spectators make a lot of noise.

Linking verbs include the forms of *be*, verbs referring to the senses (*look, feel, smell, sound, taste*), and the verbs *appear, become, grow, make, prove, remain*, and *seem*. Linking verbs do not take direct objects because these verbs do not complete an action. Instead, they link the subject with a predicate adjective or predicate nominative.

She appears happy.

Marie looks well.

There are, in English, nouns that are considered singular even though they seem to be plural (mathematics, economics), nouns that are plural in form but singular in meaning (grapes, kids), and titles of works, seemingly plural, that are single (*Cheech & Chong, Tango & Cash*). All of these, regarded as singular, take singular verbs.

Mathematics *is* an important subject.

Having kids in the house *is* fun.

Real police think *Tango & Cash is* silly.

Some nouns can be used as either singular or plural. The meaning determines the form of the verb.

Athletics *is* available to all students.
Athletics *are* difficult to continue later on.

7b   Verbs have at least three principal parts.

The three principal parts of verbs are the present form, the past form, and the past participle. For example, the principal parts of the verb *to fly* are *fly, flew, flown*. (See *Harbrace* 7b, and Glossary of Terms; *Hodges* 7a, 7b.)

Participles in Predicate   The past and present participles can be used as modifiers and can also be part of the predicate, but participles should never be used alone as the predicate of a sentence.

> John *was studying* his mathematics. [When subject causes the action, use present participle and helper.]

> Marie's room was cleaned. [When subject is affected by the action, use past participle and helper.]

7c   Tense forms express differences in time.

A verb's tense forms indicate past, present, and future, as well as the continuance or completion of the action or state of being expressed by the verb. (See *Harbrace* 7c, *Hodges* 7c.)

Present	I understand.
Present Progressive	I am understanding.
Past	I understood.
Continuing	I was understanding.
Future	I will understand.
Progressive	I will be understanding.

7d   Although rare, the subjunctive mood is still used for specific purposes.

There are three situations in which the subjunctive mood is used.

1. After *that* with verbs like *demand, recommend, urge, insist, request, suggest, move.*

   > I demand that studying *be* done.

   > We suggested that Fred *consider* moving.

2. To express wishes or (in *if* or *as if* clauses) a hypothetical, highly improbable, or contrary-to-fact condition.

   > I wish I *were* back in high school.

   > If I *were* you, I'd follow the Rangers.

3. As *had* rather than *would have* in *if* clauses expressing an imagined condition.

   > If he *had* practiced more, he would have made the team.

7e Unnecessary shifts in tense or mood can confuse readers. (See also *Harbrace* 8e; *Hodges* 23e, 27a.)

Tense shift	He *moved* into the dorm and *starts* giving orders.
Correct	He *moved* into the dorm and *started* giving orders.
Mood shift	He *should get* to know his roommate and *don't* get aggressive.
Correct	He *should get* to know his roommate and *not get* aggressive.

Verbs

NAME _____ SCORE _____

DIRECTIONS: Listed here are the infinitive (to) forms for several verbs. In the first three columns after each verb, write the verb's three principal parts (present, past, past participle). In the last column, indicate whether the verb is regular (R) or irregular (I), and transitive (TR) or intransitive (IN). Use your dictionary.

EXAMPLE

to begin	begin	began	begun	I, IN

1. to write _____ _____ _____ _____

2. to bend _____ _____ _____ _____

3. to bring _____ _____ _____ _____

4. to hear _____ _____ _____ _____

5. to learn _____ _____ _____ _____

6. to lend _____ _____ _____ _____

7. to hide _____ _____ _____ _____

8. to lie (recline) _____ _____ _____ _____

9. to see _____ _____ _____ _____

10. to tear _____ _____ _____ _____

11. to wind _____ _____ _____ _____

12. to swear _____ _____ _____ _____

13. to take _____ _____ _____ _____

14. to shake _____ _____ _____ _____

15. to creep _____ _____ _____ _____

Verbs

NAME _____ SCORE _____

DIRECTIONS: In each of the following sentences, the present participle of the sentence's verb is provided. Write the correct form of the verb in the space at the right.

EXAMPLE

I (being) here.   __am__

1. I (understanding) what   _____

   you (meaning) yesterday.   _____

2. Your books (being) in the car.   _____

3. John (passing) the test Monday   _____

   if he (studying) over the weekend.   _____

4. (Studying) for every quiz   _____

   as if it (being) a major test.   _____

5. He (working) hard last week,   _____

   and (failing) the test anyway.   _____

6. If I were you, I'd (getting) a better car   _____

   so you'll (arriving) in class on time.   _____

7. Those students (needing) help next week.   _____

8. Mary and Ed (be) cousins.   _____

9. The briefcase or the papers (be) enough   _____
   to carry.

10. Erasers or a jar of whiteout (work) on   _____
    a mistake.

11. Everybody (be) willing to work hard.   _____

12. Most of them (know) how to write.   _____

13. Statistics (be) a course required for all   _____
    psychology majors.

14. *Snow White and the Seven Dwarfs* (be) remade into a modern horror movie, and (be) on TV tonight.

    _____

    _____

15. You (regret)

    _____

    (study) when you

    _____

    (get) good grades.

    _____

Review: Coherence, Pronouns, Verbs

NAME _____ SCORE _____

DIRECTIONS: Rewrite the following paragraph. Place modifiers near the words they modify, and revise dangling modifiers. Whenever a noun is underlined, change it to an appropriate pronoun. Use the correct forms of the verbs in parentheses. You may change or add any words or phrases in order to make a coherent paragraph while keeping the sense of the original.

EXAMPLE

Walking along, John (see) the glass which was broken, so John (step) aside.

While John was walking, he saw the broken glass and stepped aside.

¹After (go) to orientation which (be) long, Marie and Joe (move) into dormitories which were far apart and a long walk away. ²Marie and Joe, after (move) Marie and Joe's luggage, (go) to the cafeteria of the school for something to eat. ³The cafeteria (be) closed so Marie and Joe (go) back to their rooms to study hungry. ⁴It (is) not encouraging for Marie and Joe their first week at college (start) this way, but things (improve) the following week. ⁵The college (have) the college's first welcoming party. ⁶Going to the party, it (be) fun for Marie and Joe and a welcome break from (study).

_____

_____

_____

_____

_____

_____

_____

_____

_____

_____

_____

_____

_____

Chapter 8

Sentence Unity: Consistency

(Hodges 23, 27) su 8

Unity actually applies to paragraphs and the entire essay as well as to sentences. In writing an essay, however, we begin with the sentence—the basic unit of written communication in English. When we speak of unity, we mean consistency—of thought and idea, purpose, organization, and structure.

8a Making the relationship of ideas in a sentence immediately clear helps the reader.

Unrelated   All colleges offer English courses but students don't like to travel too far.

Related   All colleges offer English courses, so students don't have to travel too far to find one a convenient distance from home.

8b Arranging details in a clear sequence makes your point clear.

Giving the reader too many details, especially irrelevant ones, can make your point difficult to distinguish.

Excessive   When I went to college it was in the city I was living in so I was able to take the subway and didn't have to worry about putting gas in my car or paying tolls.

Clear   I went to college near home in the city so I commuted inexpensively by subway.

8c Mixed metaphors and mixed constructions are illogical.

A metaphor is an implied comparison made up of images, verbal or portrayed. We speak metaphorically in English as a matter of course, usually without realizing it. In a popular song, for example, Frank Sinatra referred to "The autumn

Harcourt Brace & Company

of my years." He meant he's getting old. Since autumn is the third season in the annual cycle, winter in the end, the best part of his life is over.

Mixed	Still waters run along the highway of life. [Mixes *still waters run deep* and *the highway of life*.]
Revised	She lived her life keeping her emotions hidden, proving that still waters run deep.
Or	She went along the highway of life without making unnecessary stops.
Mixed	When Ed failed his science course angered the football coach. [adverbial clause, no subject of the verb *angered*]
Revised	When Ed failed his science course, he angered the football coach.
Mixed	When Cindy saw the torn book, that afternoon. [adverbial clause, noun with no predicate]
Revised	That afternoon, when Cindy saw the torn book, she went out and bought another one.

8d Faulty predication can lead to problems.

The subject and predicate must fit together logically.

Faulty	Tyrone read a book that talked about space travel. [Books don't talk.]
Revised	Tyrone read a book that covered the subject of space travel.

8e Unnecessary shifts are disconcerting.

Always try to keep tenses, person, number, mood, and level of diction (formal, informal, slang) consistent. Don't use *is when, is where,* or *is because.* They are illogical.

Faulty	Fred studying is when he gets good grades.
Revised	When Fred studies, he gets good grades.
Faulty	Carmela took the test and passed it, and Fred goes and flunks. [*goes* changes verbs and tense; *flunks* changes tone]
Revised	Carmela took the test and passed it; Fred took the test and failed it.

Harcourt Brace & Company

Sentence Unity: Consistency

Exercise 8–1

NAME _____ SCORE _____

DIRECTIONS: Rewrite the following sentences, eliminating unrelated ideas or arranging details properly.

EXAMPLE

> Juan took his algebra test last Monday and his grade came back on Tuesday, so he finished cleaning his car when he passed the test.
>
> <u>Juan passed the algebra test he took last Monday. After the test, he cleaned his car.</u>

1. When Marie went to her dormitory it was her first day of college, and even though it was raining hard, she moved into the room while she enjoyed looking at the lovely campus.

   _____

   _____

   _____

   _____

2. There are many classes offered early, but the cafeteria serves food all day.

   _____

   _____

   _____

   _____

3. Modernized versions of Shakespeare's plays are easier to understand, and the holidays are a good time for the theater and movies.

   _____

   _____

   _____

   _____

4. Carmela bought books for all her courses which were meeting early because she didn't register for any late courses and her bookcase was filled.

_____

_____

_____

_____

5. If you live in the city and go to college near home public transportation is inexpensive and you won't have to pay for room and board so you can be with your family.

_____

_____

_____

_____

Sentence Unity: Consistency   Exercise 8–2

NAME _____ SCORE _____

DIRECTIONS: Rewrite the following sentences correctly. In the space at the right, indicate whether the sentence, before you correct it, contained mixed metaphor or mixed construction (mix), faulty predication (pred), or an unnecessary shift (shift).

EXAMPLE

Fred's daydreaming got him in trouble with the instructor,
who told him to get his head out of the wrong tree.   _Mix_

Fred's daydreaming got him in trouble with the instructor, who told him to
get his head out of the clouds.

1. Marie's paper was good, but when she handed it in late.   _____

2. *The Most Dangerous Game*, by Richard Connell, kills
the villain.   _____

3. Fred was still on the wrong track, and his friends told him
he should stop barking in deep water.   _____

4. Not studying is when you get in trouble.   _____

5. Marie went to class and Juan goes to the movies.   _____

6. Carmela gave the correct answer is an example of how studying pays off.   _____

_____

_____

Chapter 9

Subordination and Coordination

(*Hodges* 24)   sub/coor 9

When we *subordinate*, we put something in a lower rank or order. When we *coordinate*, we put a thing or things in the same rank or order so that they work in harmony with one another. As we write sentences in English, we subordinate ideas of lesser importance, usually by making them dependent clauses; the main idea of the sentence is the independent clause in that sentence. If we encounter a situation where there are two or more ideas of equal importance in one sentence, we coordinate the structure of the sentence so that each idea has equal emphasis. This can be done by writing a compound sentence.

Subordination   **The final exam was given** *even though there was a storm.* [Main idea is an independent clause; subordinate clause, *even though there was a storm*, is given less emphasis in the sentence.]

Coordination   The final exam was given, *and* there was a storm. [Here are two independent clauses, and equal emphasis is given to each idea.]

9a   Careful subordination can combine a series of related short sentences into longer, more effective units.

Choppy   I went to the movies. It was Tuesday evening. The popcorn was stale. The movie was boring. I went home and studied. I never expected I'd enjoy that.

Revised   Last Tuesday I went to the movies. Not only was the movie boring, but also the popcorn was stale. I went home and studied, which I never expected I'd enjoy.

9b   Using subordination and coordination is preferable to stringing several main clauses together.

Awkward   We went to the football game last Saturday and our school's team beat the other school's team so we had a victory party but it ended early.

Revised   We went to the football game last Saturday and saw our school's team beat the other school's team. After the game, we had a victory party, which ended early.

9c   Faulty or excessive subordination can confuse the reader.

Faulty   Carol took her exams, passing all of them.

Better   After Carol took her exams, she was told she had passed all of them.

Excessive   Carol took her exams and even though they were all difficult she passed all of them, despite their difficulty, and because she studied a lot.

Better   Carol passed all her exams, despite their difficulty, because she studied a lot.

Subordination and Coordination   Exercise 9–1

NAME _____ SCORE _____

DIRECTIONS: Use subordination and coordination to combine each of the following groups of short, choppy sentences into longer, more effective sentences.

EXAMPLE

> Carmela is going to college. Her first semester starts in September. She'll commute from home. She'll carry five courses. That's fifteen credits.

> Carmela starts her first college semester in September, and will commute from home. She'll carry fifteen credits; that's five courses.

1. Cindy is going to a state college. It's near her home. She can drive to school. It's convenient. It's inexpensive. She can save money. Use that money for graduate school later.

   _____

   _____

   _____

   _____

2. All students take English in their first semester. New students take a placement test. Students who need help writing take a refresher course. It improves their writing skills.

   _____

   _____

   _____

   _____

3. Next you take literature. You can take American, British, or World Literature. They're all interesting. Be prepared to read a lot.

   _____

   _____

   _____

   _____

4. Juan is going to a private college. He wants to go away. He'll have to work part time. Otherwise he can't afford it. He can't come home every night.

_____

_____

_____

_____

5. Public or private, it's important to study. Get good grades in high school. Scholarship money helps. Home or away you need good study habits.

_____

_____

_____

_____

Subordination and Coordination

Exercise 9–2

NAME _____ SCORE _____

DIRECTIONS: The following sentences are either stringy or put together with faulty subordination or coordination. Rewrite each of them, using proper subordination or coordination or both to make effective sentences.

EXAMPLE

Ed and John have difficult schedules so they don't go to class together however they have lunch together therefore they see each other during the day.

Even though Ed and John have different schedules and don't go to class together, they do have lunch together so they see each other during the day.

1. Half of Ed's tuition is scholarship money, getting the highest grades in science in high school.

   _____

   _____

   _____

   _____

2. John worked hard to get good grades in high school but they weren't as good as Ed's, however John was a better baseball player than Ed so John got an athletic scholarship.

   _____

   _____

   _____

   _____

3. John's car broke down on the way to the big game when the home team lost.

   _____

   _____

   _____

   _____

4. Some students go to class and when they take notes they try to copy every-thing the professor says which isn't a good idea because you can't tell what's important when you go to review for a test.

_____

_____

_____

_____

_____

5. John has five courses and he plays baseball but he needs spending money therefore he wants to get a part-time job, however he won't be able to do all those things and study as much as he needs to.

_____

_____

_____

_____

_____

Harcourt Brace & Company

Chapter 10

Parallelism

(Hodges 26)   // 10

In geometry, parallel lines go in the same direction, remain the same distance apart, and never intersect. In English grammar, the principle is similar. Parallel structure in a sentence means corresponding parts all have the same structure and never conflict with one another, either in form or in meaning.

Not parallel	To *think* is **being**.
Parallel	To *think* is *to be*.
Not parallel	*Seeing* is **to believe**.
Parallel	*Seeing* is *believing*.
Not parallel	*What you see* is **what you're going to get**.
Parallel	*What you see* is *what you get*.

10a   Similar grammatical elements need to be balanced.

For a sentence to be parallel in structure, it must also be balanced—that is, parts of speech, phrases, and clauses must match.

Parallel words	The new dean is *friendly* and *happy*.
Parallel phrases	Abraham Lincoln said our government is "*of the people, by the people, and for the people.*"
Parallel clauses	We can wish for *whatever we want* and be satisfied by *whatever we get*.
Parallel sentences	I didn't like him when I met him. I liked him after I knew him.

10b   Parallels need to be clear to the reader.

We can clarify parallel structures for the reader by repetition of elements such as prepositions or articles, or the *to* of an infinitive.

> John practiced for days before the game, *in order to be ready, in order to win, in order to prove* he could do it.

> It was *the time, the place, the mood* he has always wanted.

10c   Correlatives can be used with parallel structures.

The correlative conjunctions show a grammatical relationship within a sentence. They *correlate*, that is, join elements in a sentence to make them parallel. The correlative conjunctions are *both...and, either...or, neither...nor, not only...but also*, and *whether...or*.

> Whether taking a test or playing a game, Juan is intense and focused.

> Not only does he study hard, but he also practices hard.

Parallelism   Exercise 10–1

NAME _____ SCORE _____

DIRECTIONS: Underline the parallel elements in the following sentences, and write them in the space provided.

EXAMPLE

Carol wants <u>to study</u>, <u>to do well</u>, and <u>to succeed</u>.

_____ <u>to study, to do well, to succeed</u> _____

1. Juan wanted to major in a subject that would be interesting, that would be challenging, and that would provide a career.

   _____

   _____

2. Carmela not only reads quickly, but also retains well.

   _____

   _____

3. The satisfaction one gets from writing well is in the achievement, in the knowledge, in the ability.

   _____

   _____

4. When you have free time, you can go to the cafeteria, go to the library, or go to the movies.

   _____

   _____

5. Tyrone is going to start running, swimming, and dieting.

   _____

   _____

6. Whether you stay in school or drop out is your decision; either you'll succeed in life or you'll fail depending on that decision.

   _____

   _____

Parallelism   Exercise 10–2

NAME _____ SCORE _____

DIRECTIONS: Rewrite the following sentences so that they are all parallel in structure.

EXAMPLE

I like to run, to swim, and playing football.
I like to run, to swim, and to play football.

1. College tuition is paid for by student money and publicly funded.

   _____

   _____

2. Either you spend your spare time studying unless you don't.

   _____

   _____

3. He told me that he was going to work and I should too.

   _____

   _____

4. I asked if Carmela was not only going to the game, but whether dinner also.

   _____

   _____

5. John thought it would be a good idea we all worked together, then leave together and come home in a group.

   _____

   _____

   _____

6. When we return, we can eat in the cafeteria, television or gym.

   _____

   _____

Chapter 11

Emphasis

(Hodges 29) emp 11

Whenever we communicate, whether it's a spoken or a written communication, we emphasize what we think are the important aspects of the communication. In speaking, we can raise, lower, or inflect our voices as well as use body language. In writing, however, we need to compensate for the inability to use those techniques, so we substitute subordination, coordination, parallelism, word choice, punctuation, and the like, as methods of emphasizing what we want our audience to feel is something especially important. Following are additional techniques for emphasizing.

11a Words at the beginning or end of a sentence receive emphasis.

Place important words in these positions whenever possible.

Less emphatic	Handing homework in on time is very important, according to teachers.
More emphatic	Handing homework in on time, according to teachers, is very important.

11b When surrounded by cumulative sentences, a periodic sentence receives emphasis.

In a **cumulative sentence**, the main idea comes first. In a **periodic sentence**, the main idea comes last.

Cumulative	The more you study, the higher your grades will be according to studies done by educators observing college students.
Periodic	Studies done by educators who observed college students prove that the more you study, the higher your grades will be.

11c   When ideas are arranged from least important to most important, the most important idea receives the most emphasis.

Less emphatic	The more you study, the higher your grades will be, and the higher your grades, the better job you'll get or the better your chances are of getting into graduate school, according to studies by educators.
More emphatic	According to studies done by educators, the more you study, the higher your grades will be, and the higher your grades, the better the job you'll get and the better your chances are of getting into graduate school.

11d   Forceful verbs can make sentences emphatic.

For better emphasis, use the active voice instead of the passive voice, and use action verbs instead of forms of *have* or *be*.

Passive	The first test was passed by everyone.
Active	Everyone passed the first test.
Less forceful	Our classroom has sunlight.
More forceful	The sun lights our classroom.

11e   Repeating important words gives them emphasis.

Tyrone didn't graduate by being laid-back; he *worked* for good grades, he *worked* for tuition money, he *worked* to buy his own car.

11f   Inverting the standard word order of a sentence gives it emphasis.

Less emphatic	The substantial, difficult-to-win scholarship is still available.
More emphatic	The scholarship, substantial and difficult to win, is still available.

11g Balanced sentence construction provides emphasis.

Less emphatic   Juan or Carmela could win the scholarship, but Ed and Marie don't work hard enough.

More emphatic   Juan or Carmela could win the scholarship; Ed or Marie could not win it.

11h A short sentence following one or more long ones is emphasized.

The competition for the scholarship was intense, and all the participants, although qualified, didn't seem to want to win it badly enough to work very hard. Juan did.

Emphasis   Exercise 11–1

NAME _____ SCORE _____

DIRECTIONS: Rewrite the following sentences so that they are more emphatic. In the space at the right, indicate which rule you used.

EXAMPLE

The basketball game was won by our school.

_____Our school won the basketball game._____   _11d_

1. A healthy social life and participation in sports are important parts of an education, experts will all tell you.   _____

_____

_____

_____

2. A well-balanced schedule is important, and consists of a sensible diet, sufficient exercise, and time budgeted for studying.   _____

_____

_____

3. Our school is the winner of the basketball championship.   _____

_____

_____

4. We should remember to keep our rooms neat and keep up with our laundry and car maintenance when we're in college.   _____

_____

_____

_____

5. Keep your goals in sight even though you may fail a course, or suffer some setbacks. _____

_____

_____

6. Persistence and determination are at the heart of all successful students. _____

_____

_____

7. In high school you usually had someone, a parent or a teacher, checking up on you and in college it's different. _____

_____

_____

_____

8. Faculty advisors should be consulted by students whenever there's an academic problem. _____

_____

_____

_____

9. When you apply for admission to college, the Admissions Officer will look at your academic record and participation in extracurricular activities. _____

_____

_____

_____

10. An applicant to college has his or her entire high school record examined, including participation in cultural activities, sports, and community service, and it's important to remember that. _____

_____

_____

_____

    Harcourt Brace & Company

Emphasis

NAME _____ SCORE _____

DIRECTIONS: Write a paragraph of five to seven sentences on the differences between high school and college as you perceive them to be. Each of the sentences should use one of the techniques for emphasizing presented in this chapter. Number each sentence at the beginning, and at the end put in parentheses the number of the rule you observed (See also *Harbrace* 11a through 11h; *Hodges* 29a through 29h) when writing that sentence.

_____

_____

_____

_____

_____

_____

_____

_____

_____

_____

_____

_____

_____

_____

_____

_____

_____

_____

_____

_____

_____

Chapter 12

Variety

(Hodges 30)   var 12

One of the most important aspects of good writing is the ability to keep the audience interested in what we are trying to say. Constant consideration of and for the audience is essential. Writing that is lively and imaginative, as well as structurally sound, requires that we pay attention to the rules presented in previous chapters and use a variety of sentence forms for the audience's benefit. Following are several methods writers may use to demonstrate *variety* in sentences and paragraphs.

12a A series of short, simple sentences sounds choppy. (See also *Harbrace* 11h; *Hodges* 29h.)

Choppy   Colleges have sports for men and women. The law says equal funds should go to both. Women's basketball is very popular. There's even a female goaltender in semi-pro ice hockey. Women pay tuition, too. They should get equal consideration in sports.

Effective   Colleges have coed sports programs because the law says equal funding should go to both sexes. Besides women's basketball is very popular, and there's even a female goaltender in semi-professional ice hockey. Women should get equal consideration in sports. They pay tuition, too.

12b Writing sounds monotonous when too many sentences begin the same way.

Beginning some sentences with forms or a part of speech other than the subject provides variety.

Quickly the other team took advantage of the turnover. [adverb]

With all due respect, I think the coach was wrong. [prepositional phrase]

Most teams practice all week, others don't. [coordinating conjunction or other sentence connective]

A team with history, the Packers are dominant again. [appositive]

12c   Stringing simple sentences together to make compound sentences is less effective than experimenting with sentence structure.

There are several ways to introduce variety into your sentences besides combining simple sentences into compound sentences, which merely changes your writing from choppy to monotonous.

Compound	The baseball season is long, and so are the hockey and basketball seasons, and the football season is short but exciting.
Change to complex	The football season, which isn't as long as the baseball, basketball, or hockey season, is short but exciting.
Compound predicate	Professional sports' seasons vary in length, while some excite us and others bore us.
Use an appositive	Football, the most exciting professional sport, has a shorter season than other sports.
Use a prepositional or verbal phrase	Because football is rougher and more exciting than other professional sports, its season is shorter.

12d   Occasionally using words or phrases to separate subject and verb can vary the conventional subject–verb sequence.

Subject-verb	**John won** an athletic scholarship, but he must maintain a B average.
Varied	**John,** who won an athletic scholarship, must **maintain** a B average.

12e   When surrounded by declarative sentences, a question, an exclamation, or a command adds variety.

Many people say that athletes are coddled. Others say that athletes in college aren't held to the same academic standards as other students. College administrators get blamed for this. Why? The same faculty teach athletes, don't they?

Variety

Exercise 12–1

NAME _____ SCORE _____

DIRECTIONS: Rewrite the following groups of sentences with the purpose of providing variety. Use the methods presented in this chapter. In the space at the right, indicate the particular method you are using.

EXAMPLE

John went to his room. He studied. There's a test tomorrow.

John went to his room to study because he has a test tomorrow.   12a

1. College was once only for the wealthy, but now everyone has the opportunity to go.   _____

_____

_____

_____

2. Only children of wealthy executives used to go to college. Working-class parents couldn't afford to send their children to college. Everyone has the opportunity to go to college nowadays.   _____

_____

_____

_____

3. There are state colleges and private colleges. You can go to either one. You need more money for the private ones. State schools are less expensive and just as good.   _____

_____

_____

_____

4. Applying to college is important. Applying to college can be expensive because of application fees. Applications to college should be thought out carefully before sending them. _____

_____

_____

_____

5. Plan to apply now. Pick a few colleges you like. Have your high school send a current transcript. Get your recommendations lined up. _____

_____

_____

_____

Variety

NAME _____ SCORE _____

DIRECTIONS: Here are the opening and closing sentences of a paragraph you are to complete by filling in the middle with three sentences of various constructions. Your sentences should maintain the sense of the opening sentence. Number your sentences from 2 on. After each sentence, indicate in parentheses the method you are using from *Harbrace* 12a through 12e. *(Hodges* 30a through 30e)

1. Women can play most sports as well as men, and can compete as well as men. (12a)

2. _____

   _____

   _____

3. _____

   _____

   _____

4. _____

   _____

   _____

Review: Effective Sentences

NAME _____ SCORE _____

DIRECTIONS: Rewrite the following paragraph, using the rules and techniques covered in chapters 8 through 12. Keep the sense of the paragraph, but you may change words, phrases, and clauses. You may combine sentences as well as change longer sentences to shorter ones.

[1]College has athletics, but women apply for financial aid just as men do. [2]One college believes women shouldn't play sports. [3]Another insists your grades remain high when you play. [4]Whether you take part in sports or not and you want to go to that college, however you need extra time to study, studying is more important. [5]Just remember it's important to play sports, to study hard, and keeping in touch with your family. [6]All students should be instructed by college administrators to budget their time properly. [7]Teachers know this. [8]Counselors know it, too. [9]Students and their parents should.

_____

_____

_____

_____

_____

_____

_____

_____

_____

_____

_____

_____

_____

_____

_____

_____

Chapter 13

Good Usage

When we refer to *usage* in speaking and writing, we are talking about what customary practices are in using the English language. There are levels of diction (the choice and use of words in speech and writing), and we switch from one to another depending on our audience. The three levels of diction commonly recognized in English are the *formal* level, where we strictly adhere to the forms of English grammar; the *informal* level, which we use normally in spoken language but is normally considered inappropriate for official written communications; and the *vernacular* level, which is sometimes called *slang*. Vernacular is regional and cultural, and differs from place to place as well as from culture to culture. Generally, the vernacular is an unaccepted form when used in written communication. If inserted in a piece of writing, the vernacular should be set off by quotation marks or italics.

One way of telling someone to calm down is to say, *"Hey dude, chill out."*

13a Dictionaries provide information beyond the definition of a word.

Any good, current dictionary will provide you with an explanation of the contents, individual entries, history of each word (etymology), and current usage, when appropriate, for the words being defined. Always check the introductory section and the appendices of any dictionary you intend to purchase or use. The individual entries provide you with definitions, spelling, pronunciation, and other important aspects of each word. A thesaurus can help you find synonyms.

13b Most dictionaries label words according to dialectical, regional, or stylistic usage.

Each entry will give you the level of diction for the word you are looking up.

Harcourt Brace & Company

13c   Writers consider their audience when selecting words to convey meaning and appropriate tone.

Tone refers to the way we use a word to reflect a certain meaning.

> Oh, get out of here. [said in jest, meaning "you can't be serious"]
> Get out of here! [said in anger; meant literally]

Harcourt Brace & Company

Good Usage

Exercise 13–1

NAME _____ SCORE _____

DIRECTIONS: Each of the following sentences uses informal, vernacular, or other inappropriate words or expressions. Underline those words and expressions, and using your dictionary to look up synonyms for them, rewrite the sentence in the formal level of diction.

EXAMPLE

Joe goes to the guy, "beat feet."

Joe said to the man, "get out of here."

1. He ain't got none.

_____

2. Take a chill pill, ace.

_____

3. Sit that book down on the table.

_____

4. Mankind is better off without those dopes.

_____

5. She done it without a blink.

_____

6. Why don't I lay it all out for you?

_____

7. Well, it's the bottom of the ninth, bases loaded, you're pitching, and tomorrow's your final exam.

_____

_____

8. I'm examed-out, schooled-out, and footballed-out.

_____

9. We'll be back again—*not!*

_____

10. Ask that lady cop for directions.

_____

Good Usage   Exercise 13–2

NAME _____ SCORE _____

DIRECTIONS: Buy a local newspaper (not a supermarket tabloid) and turn to the editorial page. After reading the editorials, choose ten words that are unfamiliar to you, and list them in alphabetical order in the leftmost column. Consult your dictionary, and provide the information required in each column for each word. Each word should be written with the proper syllabication.

EXAMPLE

WORD	MEANING	ORIGIN	USAGE (IF APPLICABLE)
in flect' ed	turned; altered	M.E. from Latin	—

1. _____
2. _____
3. _____
4. _____
5. _____
6. _____
7. _____
8. _____
9. _____
10. _____

Chapter 14

Exactness

(*Hodges* 20, 23e(2))   e 14

Being exact in your choice of words makes your communication, especially a written one, more understandable and complete. Choosing the precise word to suit the particular situation enables your audience to receive and understand what it is you are trying to communicate. Using denotative words, those words with explicit meanings, conveys a concrete message. Using connotative words, those words with abstract, or "outside" meanings, can enliven a written communication. Learn to use both types, but more important, learn when to use each or both. For example, the word *house* is usually defined as a structure, a dwelling. It is a denotative word. The word *home*, however, carries other meanings that are implied. A home is a structure and a dwelling, as a house is, but *home* makes us think of abstract meanings, such as family, holidays, refuge, and so on. It is a connotative word. Your dictionary is indispensable when choosing exact words.

14a   Accurate and precise word choice conveys meaning efficiently.

You should use your dictionary to determine the correct word to use. Many words seem to fit a situation, but in reality are incorrect.

> *Not exact*   Juan was *praised* for having earned good grades.
>
> *Exact*   Juan was *commended* for having earned good grades.

The connotation of *praise* is that it expresses admiration in a broad sense. The connotation of *commend* is that it expresses admiration or reward for a particular achievement.

Figurative language, language that uses words and phrases with abstract or outside meanings, is found throughout literature, especially in poetry. The occasional use of **simile** (a comparison using the word *like* or *as*) or **metaphor** (an implied comparison) can help your writing be more exact.

Simile	Tyrone was as nervous *as* a long-tailed cat in a room full of rocking chairs. [This is also a hyperbole—an exaggeration.]
Metaphor	Carmela's grandfather is in the *autumn of his life*. [He's old, just as the year is in the seasonal cycle.]

14b   Exact word choice requires an understanding of idioms.

An *idiom* is a grammatical construction peculiar to a particular language. It is understood by speakers of that language but usually does not make literal sense. That aspect of idiom makes it difficult for speakers of other languages to understand English idioms.

> Marie was *not about to* repeat a secret.

14c   Fresh expressions are more distinctive than worn-out ones.

An expression that is used excessively loses its effectiveness and become a cliché. *All-in-all,* the *bottom line,* and similar expressions that were effective when new have become clichés and should be avoided in your writing. **Euphemisms** (a milder but less precise word or term that is substituted for a more harsh term) can be awkward and misleading and at times offensive since they can be interpreted as sarcasm. *Sanitary engineer* used in place of the harsh *garbage collector* might seem more pleasant, but it is misleading.

Exactness

NAME _____ SCORE _____

DIRECTIONS: For each of the following sentences, look up each of the words in parentheses, and cross out the word whose definition is not exactly correct for that sentence. Write the correct word in the space at the right.

EXAMPLE

Parents who don't supervise their children (ab~~X~~gate, abdicate) their responsibility to the children.   _Abdicate_

1. Michael Jordan is the (pinnacle, epitome) of American sportsmanship.   _____

2. It would be to one's credit to (adapt, adopt) some of Michael's work habits.   _____

3. Most people who spend time outdoors have (hardy, hearty) constitutions.   _____

4. I tried to (recollect, remember) what the test questions were.   _____

5. Everybody on the team (agreed to, agreed about) the coach's proposal.   _____

6. Raising tuition (affects, effects) us all.   _____

7. The distribution of wealth in most countries is not (equal, equitable).   _____

8. Fred and Carmela have a (penchant, fetish) for hot, spicy food.   _____

9. The fall of your senior year in high school is the traditional time to apply for (admittance, admission) to college.   _____

10. (Thankfully, Fortunately) the game ended before the snow storm began.   _____

Exactness

Exercise 14–2

NAME _____ SCORE _____

DIRECTIONS: The following sentences contain inappropriate idioms or worn-out expressions. Underline those idioms and worn-out expressions, and rewrite the sentences with more appropriate idioms or fresh expressions. Use a dictionary or a thesaurus.

EXAMPLE

Since the Packers won the 1996 Superbowl, everyone is <u>climbing on the bandwagon.</u>

<u>Since the Packers won the 1996 Superbowl, they have more fans than an apartment house in July.</u>

1. You should shower after playing football because cleanliness is next to godliness.

    _____

    _____

    _____

    _____

2. Carmela thought she should spend less time with her boyfriend because familiarity breeds contempt and it would be a crying shame if they split up entirely.

    _____

    _____

    _____

    _____

3. The doctor told John that he'd better cool it on the drinking and driving or he'd probably kick the bucket.

    _____

    _____

    _____

    _____

4. If Marie doesn't get accepted to the college of her choice, her fall-back position is to work for a year and go to a community college, but her parents will make her face the music.

_____

_____

_____

_____

5. I'd give my eyeteeth to be one of those, you know, whatever, they make big bucks.

_____

_____

_____

_____

Chapter 15

Conciseness: Avoiding Wordiness and Needless Repetition

(*Hodges* 21, 19h)   w/rep 15

Conciseness in writing means to be brief but comprehensive. When proofreading our sentences, paragraphs, and essays, we remove unnecessary details so that we do not confuse or bore our audience.

Wordy   When Ed went to work it was raining and he was hungry but he was on time.

Concise   Ed got to work on time.

15a   Every word should count; words or phrases that add nothing to the meaning should be omitted.

Avoid redundancy (excessive detail, superfluous information), unnecessary words, and expletives (a word that signals the subject will follow the verb).

Redundant   John drove *in his car* to the game. [*in his car* is redundant]

Unnecessary words   On *the occasion of* their anniversary, they went to dinner.

Expletive   I *was of the opinion that* the party started at 8:00.

Concise   I thought the party started at 8:00.

15b   Combining sentences or simplifying phrases and clauses can eliminate needless words.

Wordy   The dormitories were red brick and three stories high and took up a whole block.

Concise   The high, red brick dormitories took up a whole block.

5. In a confrontational situation, such as a football game, one must necessarily attempt to infuse into one's psyche the mind-set of another type of person—one who reverts back to primordial roots.

_____

_____

_____

_____

Conciseness

Exercise 15–2

NAME _____ SCORE _____

DIRECTIONS: Rewrite the following paragraph using the methods for achieving conciseness presented in this chapter. Number your rewritten sentences, and at the end of each sentence, put in parentheses the number of the rule that you used to revise that sentence. (See *Harbrace* 15a through 15e, *Hodges* 21a through e, 19h.)

[1]You are writing this paragraph for the purpose of practicing to write concisely. [2]There were five rules you studied. [3]Each rule showed you a different method of achieving conciseness. [4]Each rule can help you to write better, more or less, than you were writing before you started to study the rules that helped you to write better. [5]It is incumbent upon you to endeavor to adjust your writing technique to attain an overall improvement.

_____

_____

_____

_____

_____

_____

_____

_____

_____

_____

_____

_____

_____

_____

_____

Chapter 16

Clarity and Completeness

(Hodges 22)

In chapter 15, we covered situations where too many words were used. In chapter 16, we will concern ourselves with too few words, or omitted words, which can make your writing just as unclear to a reader as too many words. When we speak, we frequently omit words, such as in "Are you going to the movies?" which becomes, when spoken, "Goin' to the movies?" The communication takes place, but in writing it is not correct structure or form, and can be misunderstood by the reader.

16a   Articles, pronouns, conjunctions, or prepositions are sometimes necessary for clarity and completeness.

Be careful not to omit any parts of speech important to the meaning of the sentence. The example in the introduction shows how a sentence can be misunderstood when a pronoun (you) is left out. The speaker could be addressing a person or a group, a friend or a stranger, and if, in speech, the inflection isn't pronounced, the sentence could be misunderstood as a statement.

Omitted article	The guard and center waited for the game to begin. [Are there two players or one?]
Correct	The guard and *the* center waited for the game to begin.
Omitted conjunction	He went to the game then went to dinner.
Correct	He went to the game, *and* then went to dinner.
Omitted preposition	The coach said he never saw that type play before.
Correct	The coach said he never saw that type *of* play before.

16b   Verbs and auxiliaries that are sometimes omitted in speech are necessary in writing to avoid awkwardness or to complete meaning.

Omitted   That was the best game I have ever seen and ever will.

Correct   That was the best game I have ever seen and ever will *see*.

16c   Complete comparisons are needed in writing to complete the meaning if it is not suggested by the context.

Incomplete   Tyrone is a better player.

Complete   Tyrone is a better player than his cousin.

Informal   Tyrone will need a lot of help.

Complete   In Friday's game, Tyrone will need a lot of help. [completed by context]

16d   The intensifiers *so, such*, and *too* need a completing phrase or clause.

Informal   Tyrone is such a player.

Formal   Tyrone is such a good player that other teams are envious.

Clarity and Completeness

Exercise 16–1

NAME _____ SCORE _____

DIRECTIONS: Rewrite each of the following sentences, adding any omitted words and giving the sentence a sense of clarity and completeness. In the space at the right, indicate which rule you are applying. (See *Harbrace* 16a through 16d; *Hodges* 22a through 22d.)

EXAMPLE

John and friend played ball

_____ John and a friend played ball. _____   16a

1. Ed is smarter.   _____

2. Practice will be at 3:00 p.m.   _____

3. He is quick and his foul shot good.   _____

4. Freddy is such fun.   _____

5. That's too much.   _____

6. The crowd at the game has never and never will be noisier.   _____

7. Fred and Marie went to the restaurant, ate dinner.   _____

8. We won't go those people.   _____

9. The Packers scored more.   _____

10. The game was long and the crowd tired.   _____

Clarity and Completeness   Exercise 16–2

NAME _____ SCORE _____

DIRECTIONS: Rewrite the following paragraph, inserting the omitted articles, conjunctions (including any missing subordinating conjunctions), verbs, and prepositions.

My brother and I went two ballgames last season. The first game we attended was better, probably because our team won and I almost caught a fly ball. The second game was less eventful, but I get to eat hot dog and some the peanuts they sell in the stands. (My brother ate rest.) And even though our team didn't win the second game, my brother I had much fun, just being together, we are planning two more trips to ballpark this season.

Review: Diction

NAME _____ SCORE _____

DIRECTIONS: Rewrite the following paragraph, applying the rules for good diction covered in chapters 13 through 16. (See *Hodges* 19 through 22.) Pay special attention to the words and phrases underlined. Look them up in a dictionary or thesaurus.

[1]We went to the game happy but didn't want to <u>provoke</u> the other team. [2]They had some <u>dopey</u> fans who just <u>don't get it</u>. [3]We <u>set</u> ourselves down and watched the game <u>unfold</u>. [4]We paid a lot for the seats, <u>and</u> they were good seats. [5]Our team kept going after the other team <u>persistently</u>. [6]The stadium was as <u>busy as a classroom</u>, and the hot dog vendor was <u>selling out like hotcakes</u>. [7]He was a <u>dynamic</u>. [8]In the fourth quarter it started to rain <u>cats and dogs</u>, and I thought the other team would <u>bite the dust</u>. [9]It was <u>a crying shame</u>, and it was <u>a bitter-tasting pill</u> for them to swallow. [10]Our team won <u>by means of</u> scoring six touchdowns to the other team's scoring only two <u>six-point</u> touchdowns. [11]Our team won and we were happy that our team won. [12]Our team outplayed the other team. [13]It was a culmination of excessive adrenaline flowing during the game and a complete program of physical training culminating in a high level of preparedness. [14]It was good lesson for everyone, and very satisfying to us. [15]They're so good.

_____

_____

_____

_____

_____

_____

_____

_____

_____

_____

_____

_____

Chapter 17

The Comma

(*Hodges* 12, 13)   , 17

When we communicate verbally, we have the ability to use voice inflections and body language to assist in conveying meaning and emphasis. We can use our hands and facial expressions, pause, raise or lower our voices—any number of methods or devices that supplement our words in helping our audience understand us. Those "methods" can't be used in writing, however, so we have to find another way to compensate for the inability to use body language and vocal inflections. That way, or method, is the use of punctuation. The five chapters on punctuation, beginning with the comma, are designed to help you supplement your sentence construction when communicating in writing.

17a Commas come before a coordinating conjunction that links independent clauses.

My senior year in high school seemed to last forever, and it's already time to begin college.

The placement test was easy, but I studied for it anyway.

17b A comma usually follows introductory words, phrases, and clauses.

Clause   When you take notes during a lecture, write down only what's important.

Phrase   Off the record, I don't agree with her.

Introductory No, I did not enjoy the badminton class.
word

17c Commas separate items in a series (including coordinate adjectives).

Words	The test was long, difficult, and tiring.
Phrases	John went from his car, to the cafeteria, into the kitchen.
Clauses	If you feel tired, if you feel depressed, or if you feel like quitting, call home for support.
Coordinate adjectives	It is a large, colorful, beautiful campus. [Two or more adjectives modify the same noun.]

17d Commas set off nonrestrictive and other parenthetical elements, as well as contrasted elements, items in dates, and so on.

Nonrestrictive clauses	One of the most important things to remember about college, *and there are several important things to remember*, is that you are responsible for turning assignments in on time.
Contrasted element	My counselor said the desire to become an educated person, *not the hope of getting a better job*, should be the main reason I go to college.
Geographical names, dates, addresses	The U.S. Marine Corps was founded on November 10, 1775, at Tun Tavern, Philadelphia.

17e Commas are occasionally needed for ease in reading.

No comma	Those who want to go to the movies.
Comma inserted	Those who want to, go to the movies.

17f Unnecessary (or misplaced) commas send false signals that can confuse a reader.

Unnecessary	He said, to go home early would be good.
More clear	He said to go home early would be good.
Unnecessary	I did my studying, and, went to sleep.
More clear	I did my studying, and went to sleep.
Unnecessary	We did extra studying for science courses, such as, biology.
More clear	We did extra studying for science courses, such as biology.

The Comma   Exercise 17–1

NAME _____ SCORE _____

DIRECTIONS: The following sentences contain excess or misplaced commas, or necessary commas are missing. Rewrite the sentences with correct comma form, and write the rule or rules applied in the space at the right.

EXAMPLE

If, you go to the store buy me a newspaper.

_____If you go to the store, buy me a newspaper._____   __17f__

1. When you speak speak clearly.   _____

   _____

2. Marie went to the bookstore and also, stopped for a soda. _____

   _____

3. Those who want to may write an extra paper.   _____

   _____

4. Carmela, called her mother who was at work.   _____

   _____

5. Her mother who got the message called back.   _____

   _____

6. The phone rang and rang until Marie answered it.   _____

   _____

7. Marie's mother is understanding responsive and generous. _____

   _____

8. When you want to study when you want to go to the
   movies and when you want to go home all at the same
   time you must consider your priorities.   _____

   _____

   _____

9. The test which took two hours to finish wasn't that difficult. _____

_____

10. I finished the test, and, went to the movies. _____

_____

The Comma

NAME _____ SCORE _____

DIRECTIONS: Rewrite the following paragraph, inserting commas where necessary, and omitting unnecessary commas.

[1]As I see it college is quite different from high school in many respects and, similar in many others. [2]The major difference, I found is in the area of personal responsibility. [3]Your teacher your counselor your parents no one in fact is there, to stand over you to make you or remind you to do your work or take care of your laundry or make your meals and so forth. [4]This could be good or, bad depending on your personality. [5]With that in mind make your own decision about whether to go to college, near home or away from home.

_____
_____
_____
_____
_____
_____
_____
_____
_____
_____
_____
_____
_____
_____
_____
_____
_____
_____

Chapter 18

The Semicolon

(*Hodges* 14)   ; 18

A semicolon acts as a coordinator and is used between independent clauses that are related in idea. It is stronger than a comma. It can join independent clauses in situations that, if a comma were used, would constitute a comma splice. (See also *Harbrace* 3; *Hodges* 3.)

18a   Semicolons connect independent clauses not linked by a coordinating conjunction.

Certain sports are exciting; others aren't; I don't like boring sports. [ideas closely related]

Certain sports are exciting, and others aren't, but I don't like boring sports. [less closely related]

Certain sports are exciting. Others aren't. I don't like boring sports. [separate ideas]

Certain sports are exciting; however, others aren't. [conjunctive adverb between independent clauses]

18b   Semicolons separate elements that themselves contain commas.

The library has research material for literature, science, and other subjects; use it frequently, but correctly.

18c   Semicolons do not connect parts of unequal grammatical rank.

Incorrect   I played football; a rough sport.

Correct   I played football, a rough sport.

or

I played football; it's a rough sport.

The Semicolon   Exercise 18–1

NAME _____ SCORE _____

DIRECTIONS: Rewrite the following sentences using semicolons whenever they are appropriate, or eliminating them where inappropriate. In the space at the right, indicate the rule that applied. If the sentence is correct, write C in the space.

EXAMPLE

I took my car to school, it broke down.

<u>   I took my car to school; it broke down.   </u>   <u> 18a </u>

1. I like my car; the gas-guzzler.   _____

2. We went to the game, to the library, and to the cafeteria, we were tired and hungry.   _____

3. Some games are high scoring some games are low scoring.   _____

4. There are two subjects I really like; history and biology.   _____

5. Fred, Juan, Marie, and Ed went to the movies; Tyrone and Carmela, who don't like movies, went to the gym.   _____

6. Marie likes the Astros in baseball, Juan likes the Bears in football, Ed likes the Rangers in hockey, I don't agree with any of them.   _____

The Semicolon   Exercise 18–2

NAME _____ SCORE _____

DIRECTIONS: Rewrite the following sentences inserting semicolons or commas where appropriate.

1. The heater in our dormitory room is broken consequently we have to bundle up.

   _____

   _____

2. We finally painted the hall it took all day.

   _____

   _____

3. The readings for this class were written by Toni Morrison the novelist Emily Dickinson the poet and Tennessee Williams the playwright.

   _____

   _____

   _____

4. She is late to class every day however she usually comes prepared.

   _____

   _____

5. On New Year's Eve I made two resolutions exercise and eat right.

   _____

   _____

6. I receive catalogs from J. Crew and L.L. Bean which sell clothing Paper Direct which sells stationery and the Potterybarn which offers items for interior design.

   _____

   _____

   _____

7. Today my English class met in the computer lab we used the computers to write and send e-mail messages.

_____

_____

_____

8. Some people relax to music others watch television I enjoy both.

_____

_____

9. I broke his favorite coffee mug the yellow and blue one.

_____

_____

10. Nina needed to leave the concert early otherwise she would miss her nephew's birthday party.

_____

_____

_____

Chapter 19 | The Apostrophe

(*Hodges* 15)   ' 19

The function of the apostrophe is to show possession (except for personal pronouns), to indicate where there are missing elements (letters, words) in contractions, and to make the singular of certain words into the plural. For local and current usage, consult your dictionary.

19a   The apostrophe shows possession for nouns (including acronyms such as NASA) and indefinite pronouns (*everyone, everybody*).

Noun	Fred's car broke down.
Acronym	NASA's last flight was a success.
Indefinite pronoun	Everybody's lights went off.
Endings of s, x, or z sound	Phyllis' car is red. [Do not repeat *s*.]
Plural nouns	The men's dormitory is being painted.
Plural nouns ending in s	All the boys' lockers were opened.
Joint ownership	Marie and Carmela's car is blue.
Individual ownership	Fred's and John's cars are different.

19b   The apostrophe marks omissions in contractions and numbers.

I don't (do not) think so!

We'll (we will) decide that.

We're (we are) the class of '99 (1999).

19c   The apostrophe and -s form certain plurals.

The instructions give you the a's, b's, and c's of assembly.

There are many plus's to that. [word referred to as a word]

19d   Personal pronouns and plural nouns that are not possessive do not take an apostrophe.

Personal pronouns have their own forms to show possession (my, mine, our, ours, your, yours, his, her, hers, its, their, theirs).

Personal pronouns	You have *yours* and I have *mine*.
Plural noun	They went to the Smiths. [plural noun, not possessive]

The Apostrophe

Exercise 19–1

NAME _____ SCORE _____

DIRECTIONS: Rewrite the following sentences adding an apostrophe wherever needed. Write the rule or rules that apply in the space at the right.

EXAMPLE

Its a small favor to ask.

_____It's a small favor to ask._____   __19b__

1. Thats not his, its mine.   _____

2. Johns car and Eds are the same year.   _____

3. Doesnt she realize shes wrong?   _____

4. In that English class, you have to watch your ps and qs.   _____

5. Whose brother is it whos making the complaint?   _____

6. Its not the right time for that kind of question.   _____

7. The ASPCA record of helping stray dogs and cats find homes is its best attribute.   _____

8. Bad weather has an effect on everybodys comfort.   _____

9. His grade sheet has three plus and two minus. _____

_____

10. Thats mine and the other is the Smiths. _____

_____

Harcourt Brace & Company

The Apostrophe

Exercise 19–2

NAME _____ SCORE _____

DIRECTIONS: Rewrite the following paragraph, inserting apostrophes when needed.

Stacey and Barbaras favorite pastime is going to the art museum. Staceys time in the museum is spent studying Monets and Van Goghs paintings. She loves the museums collection of impressionist art. Unlike Stacey, Barbara isnt interested in the Impressionists work. Barbara spends her time viewing the new exhibits, such as mummies treasures, womens photography, and 20s memorabilia.

_____

_____

_____

_____

_____

_____

_____

_____

_____

_____

_____

_____

_____

_____

_____

_____

_____

Chapter 20

Quotation Marks

(Hodges 16)   "" 20

Quotation marks are always used in pairs. The first mark is used at the beginning of the quotation, and the second mark is used at the end of the quotation.

20a   Quotation marks set off direct questions and dialogue.

Direct quote	"Dedicated to the proposition," states the Declaration of Independence, "that all men are created equal."
Indirect quote	The Declaration of Independence states that all men are created equal. [no quotation marks required.]
Quotation within quotation	"Ed told me, 'no, I won't go,' so I left him alone," I said to Marie.
Dialogue—quoted conversations	"Do you understand this play?" asked the coach.
Thoughts	"That coach must think I'm crazy," Eddy thought.

20b   Long quotations are indented.

Any time you are quoting from a text, you will probably follow either the Modern Language Association (MLA) style (see *Harbrace* 34a; *Hodges* 38a) or the American Psychological Association (APA) style (see *Harbrace* 34d; *Hodges* 38d). When quoting poetry, a quotation of up to three lines may be included in the text, using the slash to distinguish lines of poetry (see *Harbrace* 21h; *Hodges* 17h). When quoting more than three lines, set the lines off, double spaced and indented ten spaces, and follow the spacing and punctuation of the poem.

20c   Quotation marks enclose the titles of short works such as stories, essays, poems, songs, episodes of a radio or television series, articles in periodicals, and subdivisions of books.

Short story	"The Guest" by Camus is an excellent short story.
Poem	"My Mistress' Eyes" by Shakespeare is an example of a satirical poem.
Song	When the Stones sing "Satisfaction" nowadays, it seems ironically appropriate.
TV show	"Brooklyn South" seems exaggerated, but it isn't.
Article in periodical	Did you read, "How to Help Your Aging Parents" in *Woman's Day?*

20d   Used sparingly, quotation marks may enclose words intended in a special or ironic sense.

The "mother of all parties" that Joe and Fran hosted was a complete dud.

20e   Overusing quotation marks detracts from readability.

Overuse	He knows he has to "do the right thing." [It is unnecessary to highlight a cliché.]
Overuse	I'll have to say "yes" to that offer. [Yes or no in indirect discourse do not need quotes.]

20f   Follow American printing conventions for using various marks of punctuation with quoted material.

The period and the comma are usually placed inside the quotation marks, whereas the semicolon and colon are placed outside the quotation marks. The dash, the question mark, and the exclamation point are placed inside the quotation marks when they apply to what is being quoted, and outside the quotation marks when they apply to the whole sentence.

Comma and period   "Marie," John said, "I passed chemistry."

Semicolon and colon   We were discussing "symbolism in fantasy"; I recalled what Hawthorne did in "Young Goodman Brown": he used the woods and names.

Question mark,
exclamation point,
dash—

    Inside   Fred asked, "What time is it?"

           I answered, "Look yourself!"

           "You won't answer a simple—" he paused, upset, "question?"

   Outside   What do you mean by "jumbo shrimp"?

           So this is what you mean by "the fast track"!

           She must have been expecting me to say "no, there's something better."—I guess.

Quotation Marks

Exercise 20–1

NAME _____ SCORE _____

DIRECTIONS: Rewrite the following sentences, placing the proper quotation marks where they are needed. In the space at the right, indicate the rule that applies. If the sentence is correctly punctuated and does not need any quotation marks, write C in the space at the right.

EXAMPLE

Get out of here, said the angry bartender.

"Get out of here," said the angry bartender.   20a

1. Eddy told me to get my act together, according to Freddy.   _____

2. Eddy said get your act together, said Fred.   _____

3. Born in the USA was a hit for The Boss, Bruce Springsteen.   _____

4. David Caruso began his career starring in N.Y.P.D. Blue on television.   _____

5. You should say no to offers that claim to make easy money.   _____

6. His claim to have the deal of a lifetime should have made you suspicious.   _____

7. Carmela, Marie said, why don't we go to the movies tonight?   _____

8. What do you mean when you say I've had it? _____

_____

9. I mean he's stupid, not intellectually challenged. _____

_____

10. You get what you pay for, my father says, and you pay for
    what you get. _____

_____

_____

Quotation Marks

Exercise 20–2

NAME _____ SCORE _____

DIRECTIONS: Rewrite the following sentences, adding any needed quotation marks.

1. He quickly asked, How do you download a file from the Internet?

_____

_____

2. My roommate hums The Yellow Rose of Texas all day long.

_____

_____

3. Samuel shouted How could you leave me here alone!

_____

_____

4. My favorite short story is Kate Chopin's The Storm.

_____

_____

5. When I was younger, he said, I could easily run 5 miles a day.

_____

_____

6. How do you pronounce the word mezzanine?

_____

_____

7. I would rather stay home and watch X Files than go to a movie.

_____

_____

8. His infamous thirty-foot yacht turned out to be a fishing boat.

_____

_____

9. Before writing her critique of the short story, Margarita read an essay titled Imagery in Steinbeck's Chrysanthemums.

_____

_____

_____

10. Our professor asked my group to define the literary term Petrarchan sonnet; we explained to her that it refers to a particular type of fourteen-line poem, such as Robert Frost's poem Design.

_____

_____

_____

Chapter 21

The Period and Other Marks

(Hodges 17)

pom 21

Several more punctuation marks will be covered in this chapter. Most of them have specialized functions that you should become familiar with. The uses of the hyphen are covered in *Harbrace* 22f, *Hodges* 18f. Your dictionary will contain the current rules governing use of the period.

21a   Periods punctuate certain sentences and abbreviations.

Declarative	We all have to learn to work together.
Mild imperative	Let's work together.
After some abbreviations	Dr. E. Jones has a son named E. Jones, Jr.

21b   The question mark occurs after direct (but not indirect) questions.

Direct	Where is Juan?
Indirect	Someone is looking for Juan.
Incorrect	They asked him where is Juan.
Correct	"Where is Juan?" they asked.

21c   The exclamation point occurs after an emphatic interjection and after other expressions to show strong emotion, such as surprise or disbelief.

Whoa! Knock it off!

"Look out!" he yelled. [no comma after direct quotation]

21d The colon calls attention to what follows and separates time and scriptural references and titles and subtitles.

Calling attention	The coach wanted three things: loyalty, devotion, and teamwork.
Time references	The game begins at 12:30 p.m.
Title and subtitle	Mary Shelley wrote *Frankenstein: The New Prometheus.*
After the salutation in a business letter	Dear Professor Jacobs:

21e The dash marks a break in thought, sets off a parenthetical element for emphasis or clarity, and sets off an introductory series.

A dash consists of two hyphens joined together.

Sudden break in thought	John was tired—who isn't?
Parenthetical element	Other teams in the league—who need talent and experience—hire free agents.
Introductory series	Rested, well trained, well fed—I was ready for the big game.

21f Parentheses set off nonessential matter and enclose characters used for enumeration.

First-time use of acronym	The Scholastic Aptitude Test (SAT) is used by most Eastern colleges as an admission standard.
Enumeration	The coach said that once the game started we should (1) play hard, (2) play smart, (3) play well.
Nonessential matter	Women are just as capable as men (studies have demonstrated) in the sciences.

21g   Brackets set off interpolations in quoted matter and replace parentheses within parentheses.

One of the all-time great baseball players, "Joltin' Joe" [DiMaggio] was born in San Francisco.

21h   The slash occurs between terms to indicate that either term is applicable and also marks line divisions in quoted poetry.

Unspaced between terms	Television programs today attempt to appeal to viewers through the use of violence and/or foul language.
Spaces between lines of poetry	Poe's *The Fall of the House of Usher* begins with two lines of poetry from Bérauger: "His heart is a suspended lute; / Whenever one touches it, it responds."

21i   Ellipsis points (three equally spaced periods) mark an omission from a quoted passage or a reflective pause or hesitation.

Omission within a quoted sentence	Jean-Paul Sartre notes that "As for the play, what troubles me is . . . the ending." [Sartre commenting on Arthur Miller's *The Crucible*]
Omission at beginning	Sartre notes that "what troubles me is the ambiguity of the ending." [no ellipsis or capitals]
Omission at end	Sartre notes that "As for the play, what troubles me is the ambiguity . . . ." [one period added for ending sentence]
Omission of a sentence or more	Sartre notes that "As for the play, what troubles me is the ambiguity of the ending . . . and that everything boils down to the same thing."
Reflective pause	I went to a state college instead of a private college. I wonder what would have happened . . . .

The Period and Other Marks   Exercise 21–1

NAME _____ SCORE _____

DIRECTIONS: Rewrite the following sentences, placing the correct punctuation marks where needed. Indicate the rule you have applied in the space at the right. If the sentence is correctly punctuated, write C in the space.

EXAMPLE

What does Ed think he's doing.

<u>What does Ed think he's doing?</u>   <u>21b</u>

1. Classes begin at 9:00 a.m. on Monday   _____

2. They wanted to know what Ed was doing.   _____

3. Holy smoke. That's something.   _____

4. Ice hockey a fast and rough sport is becoming very popular.   _____

5. The stadium was just what I thought it would be large, windy, and expensive.   _____

6. Dear Senator Johnson Thank you for recommending me to the Service Academy.   _____

7. Anyone in this country can if he or she wants to become successful.   _____

8. When you have a choice, it's referred to as an either or situation.

   _____

   _____

   _____

9. Anytime he Jim Brown got the ball, the other team worried.

   _____

   _____

   _____

10. Auto-Immune Deficiency Syndrome AIDS is a twentieth century nightmare.

   _____

   _____

   _____

Harcourt Brace & Company

The Period and Other Marks

Exercise 21–2

NAME _____ SCORE _____

DIRECTIONS: Rewrite the following paragraphs, applying the principles of punctutation discussed in *Harbrace* 21a through 21f and 17; *Hodges* 17a through 17f and 12.

Recently my class went to the library to research our essay topics I had chosen to write about the Internet But I wasn't sure where to begin my research so I asked the reference librarian for help Excuse me could you tell me where I might find information on the Internet I asked her She replied Are you looking for information that is actually on the Internet or just information about the Internet I stood stunned apparently I needed to think about this a bit more but soon I decided that information about the Internet printed or online would be best

So the librarian showed me several helpful periodicals the *New York Times Time Newsweek* and *Internet World* She then left me with these final works If you need more help after you have narrowed your topic just let me know I was able to narrow my topic and find plenty of articles addressing it Now when I go to the library I always stop by to say Hi to the librarian who helped me.

Harcourt Brace & Company

Review: Punctuation

NAME _____ SCORE _____

DIRECTIONS: Rewrite the following paragraph with the proper punctuation added.

[1]Now that we have covered parts of speech sentences and punctuation you should be prepared supposedly to move on to more challenging material, such as paragraphs and essays [2]Are you [3]If so be patient [4]First you must master before you move on mechanics spelling capitals italics etc [5]Once thats done youll put together paragraphs and essays [6]You should review whats been covered build on what youve learned then move on to the next level [7]Be patient be persistent [8]Once you finish this book you should be able to produce written communications that are superior to what you were producing way back when

_____

_____

_____

_____

_____

_____

_____

_____

_____

_____

_____

_____

_____

_____

_____

_____

Chapter 22

Spelling, the Spell Checker, and Hyphenation

(*Hodges* 18)   s/sp/h 22

Spelling can be a major problem for students of English. The language does not always lend itself to the following of phonetics. Many words in English aren't spelled the way they sound. An example of this is *though*, along with many other words with *gh* in them, as with *thought* and *tough*.

Computers can be helpful but shouldn't cause students to become overconfident or complacent since a computer with *Spell Check*, for example, won't pick up on a correctly spelled word that is misused, as with *affect* for *effect*, or *principal* for *principle*. Besides, you won't always have your computer with you when you write.

Use your dictionary while you write and when you proofread. This doesn't cover all situations either, since you won't know to look up a word if you don't know it's misspelled, and you won't have time to look up every word when you write in class. Increasing your vocabulary and correcting the vocabulary you already have can be done by the regular reading of correct English, whether it be fiction, biography, technical writing, newspapers, or news magazines. Television won't do it. Personal tricks or codes that work for you can help. For example, remembering the rhyme, "I before e / except after c / or when sounded like a / as in neighbor and weigh," can solve many spelling problems (see *Harbrace* 22e, *Hodges* 18e).

22a Spelling often does not reflect pronunciation.

The best way to check the pronunciation of a word is to consult your dictionary. Learn how English vowels are pronounced, become familiar with difficult or unusual situations, such as *gh* mentioned in the introduction, and pronounce words as they are spelled (phonetically). If a word doesn't sound right when read phonetically, check the spelling. This procedure won't always work in reverse. If you write phonetically, you will misspell words such as *might* and *jewelry*. Learn the phonetic alphabet, a key to pronunciation. You will find it in most standard dictionaries.

22b When words sound alike but have different meanings, the spelling determines the meaning.

Words that sound alike but have different meanings are called **homophones**. Examples are *forth* and *fourth*, *sail* and *sale*, *it's* and *its*, *their*, *there*, and *they're*, and many others. A spell checker will not point out words based on their functions in a sentence. Remember, there is no shortcut to correct spelling. Use your dictionary, and study definitions of words whose spelling you look up. You will learn to associate meaning with spelling, and cut down on spelling errors by knowing when to use the correct spelling of a homophone. For a comprehensive list of homophones, see *Harbrace* 22b, *Hodges* 18b.

22c Adding a prefix to a base word changes the meaning.

A prefix is an addition in front of the base (root) word, with no letter dropped or added. A spell checker will usually detect misspellings.

happy, unhappy

competent, incompetent

22d Adding a suffix may require changing the spelling of the base word.

A suffix is an addition to the end of the base (root) word, and it can affect the spelling of the word. A spell checker will usually detect misspellings. Whenever you add a suffix, or use a word whose base you know how to spell but are unsure of the spelling with the suffix added, consult your dictionary. Frequently, the word will be part of the listing for the base word.

22e *Ei* and *ie* are often confused.

Refer to the short rhyme in the introduction to this chapter. When the sound is *e* as in *me*, use *ie* except after *c*, when you use *ei*. When the sound is *ay*, use *ei*.

Me sound	chief, yield
After c	receive, perceive
Ay sound	weigh, eight
Exceptions	either, neither, friend, species, foreign

22f Hyphens both link and divide words.

Hyphens bring together two or more words that function as a single word, and they divide words at the end of a line.

Linking words	Who is this Johnny-come-lately? [noun] Double-check your spelling. [verb]
Multiple adjectives	The coach has a well-thought-out plan.
Spelled-out fractions	He isn't one-half the man his father was.
Compound numbers, *twenty-one to ninety-nine*	He's only twenty-one years old. She's having her twenty-seventh birthday.
Between prefix or suffix *and root*	Have them re-sign the contract. [*resign* would be ambiguous]
Prefixes ex-, self-, all-	Her ex-boyfriend showed up. He's a self-made success. He thinks he's all-knowing.
Suffix -elect	John is the captain-elect of the hockey team.
Prefix with a capitalized *word*	There are thousands of ex-New Yorkers who moved west.

There are several guidelines for dividing a word at the end of a line.

Don't divide abbreviations, initials, capitalized acronyms, or one-syllable words.

> *Examples*   a.m. NOT a.-m.   USMC NOT US-MC   tough NOT tou-gh

Don't create one-letter syllables (even though you may see this done in newspapers).

> *Example*   o-mit *or* omi-t

Divide hyphenated words only at the hyphen.

> *Examples*   brother-/in-/law   anti-/drugs

Divide words between two consonants that come between vowels—except when the division doesn't reflect pronunciation.

> *Examples*   pic-/nic   dis-/cuss   BUT   co-bra

Divide words between those consonants that double when adding *-ing*.
> *Examples*   set-/ting   plan-/ning

Misspelling because of Mispronunciation   Exercise 22–1

NAME _____ SCORE _____

DIRECTIONS: The following words are frequently misspelled. Look up each word in your dictionary. In the first column, write the correct syllabication with primary accent. In the second column, write the first meaning (definition) given.

EXAMPLE

Absence   <u>ab'-sence</u>   <u>The state of being away</u>

1. accessible _____ _____

2. accommodate _____ _____

3. acquire _____ _____

4. across _____ _____

5. advise _____ _____

6. arrangement _____ _____

7. benefited _____ _____

8. cafeteria _____ _____

9. competence _____ _____

10. conscience _____ _____

11. desirable _____ _____

12. disastrous _____ _____

13. exaggerate _____ _____

14. extraordinary _____ _____

15. fascinate _____ _____

16. grammar _____ _____

17. legitimate _____ _____

18. mischievous _____ _____

19. opportunity _____ _____

20. privilege _____ _____

21. quiet   _____   _____

22. rhythm   _____   _____

23. similar   _____   _____

24. stubbornness   _____   _____

25. surprise   _____   _____

26. through   _____   _____

27. unconscious   _____   _____

28. villain   _____   _____

29. weather   _____   _____

30. writing   _____   _____

Confusion of Words of Similar Sound or Spelling

Exercise 22–2

NAME _____ SCORE _____

DIRECTIONS: In the following sentences, cross out the word whose meaning is incorrect for that sentence. Write the correct word in the space at the right. Consult your dictionary for each word's meaning.

EXAMPLE

She would not (accept, ex̶c̶ept) his gift.   _accept_

1. The first meal in that restaurant was with the (complements, compliments) of the house.   _____

2. The first show was sold out, and the (aisles, isles) were full of people.   _____

3. (Gorilla, Guerilla) warfare was being waged in the mountains.   _____

4. He was (formerly, formally) given notice to leave.   _____

5. The cowboy (rode, road) the wild (horse, hoarse) until it calmed down.   _____

6. Use the proper (stationary, stationery) to write a letter to a friend.   _____

7. Finally, some (piece, peace) of mind.   _____

8. I'll give him a (piece, peace) of my mind.   _____

9. I'm more angry (than, then) he is.   _____

10. This is a (personal, personnel) issue between us, so none of the office's (personal, personnel) need get involved.   _____

11. The doctor's (patience, patients) is at an end.   _____

12. The (principle, principal) involved is an ethical one, and the (principle, principal) will have to resolve it.   _____

Prefixes and Suffixes   Exercise 22–3

NAME _____   SCORE _____

DIRECTIONS: In the space at the right, enter the correct spelling of each word after adding the prefix or suffix as indicated. Use your dictionary.

EXAMPLE

un + necessary   <u>unnecessary</u>

argue + able   <u>arguable</u>

1. mis + understand   _____

2. mis + spent   _____

3. re + evaluate   _____

4. use + age   _____

5. excite + able   _____

6. advantage + ous   _____

7. write + ing   _____

8. manage + ment   _____

9. judge + ment   _____

10. stop + ing   _____

11. defy + ance   _____

12. try + es   _____

13. hungry + ly   _____

14. donkey + s   _____

15. accompany + es   _____

Hyphenated Words

Exercise 22–4

NAME _____ SCORE _____

DIRECTIONS: Rewrite the following sentences with the correct hyphenation added.

EXAMPLE

He was a well meaning person.

He was a well-meaning person.

1. The ex captain of the New York Rangers is Mark Messier.

_____

_____

_____

2. In order to pass any financial plans in our ultra conservative homeowner's association, a two thirds majority is needed.

_____

_____

_____

3. It's not as though we live in a high rise apartment in the city; we're quasi rural.

_____

_____

_____

4. All the houses were well built in the mid 1940s and 1950s.

_____

_____

_____

5. The people who built the community were hard boiled immigrants from old world Europe.

_____

_____

_____

6. If I had one half their energy nowadays, I'd consider myself lucky.

_____

_____

_____

Chapter 23 | Capitals

(*Hodges* 9)

There are many rules covering capitalization in English. Whenever you are unsure whether or not to capitalize in a particular situation, it is best to consult a recently published dictionary.

23a Proper names are capitalized and so usually are their abbreviations and acronyms (words formed from the initial letters or parts of a word).

1. Names and nicknames of persons or things and trademarks

    James Baldwin, Sting, World Series, Sprite

2. People and their languages

    New Englanders, Native Americans, Russian

3. Geographical names

    South America, Broadway, Washington Monument

4. Organizations, government agencies, institutions, and companies

    Green Bay Packers, Federal Bureau of Investigation, National Rifle Association, Shell Oil Company

5. Days of the week, months, and holidays

    Friday, October, Christmas

6. Historical documents, periods, events, and movements

    Bill of Rights, Medieval, The Revolution, Realism

7. Religions and their adherents, holy books, holy days, and words denoting the Supreme Being

   Christianity, Christian; Judaism, Jew, Islam, Muslim
   Bible, Koran, Talmud
   Easter, Ramadan, Yom Kippur
   God, Allah, Yahweh, Buddha, Vishnu

8. Personifications (when human characteristics are attributed to a nonhuman, such as an object or a concept)

   Their house was visited by Sadness.

9. Words derived from proper names

   Napoleonic [adjective]; Westernize [verb]

10. Abbreviations and acronyms or shortened forms of capitalized words

    MADD, NHL, Washington, D.C.

23b   Titles of persons that precede the name are capitalized but not those that follow it or stand alone.

President Bill Clinton; Bill Clinton, president

23c   In titles and subtitles of books, plays, essays, and other titled works, the first and last words are capitalized, as well as most other words.

"Buffy, the Vampire Slayer"
"N.Y.P.D. Blue"
"The Good, the Bad, and the Ugly"

23d   The pronoun *I* and the interjection *O* are capitalized.

If it were I, O goodness, I wouldn't forget.

The interjection *oh* is not capitalized except when it begins a sentence.

23e The first word of every sentence (or of any other unit written as a sentence) and of directly quoted speech is capitalized.

"It ain't over," Yogi Berra said, "until it's over."
OR
Yogi Berra said, "It ain't over until it's over."

23f Capitals sometimes indicate emphasis.

Professional hockey players who compete for the Stanley Cup are driven by Pride.

23g Unnecessary capitals are distracting.

Always capitalize proper nouns, but not common nouns when preceded by the indefinite articles *a* and *an* or by modifiers like *every* or *several*.

A history course is worth taking.

Every college offers several.

Every American should stand during the playing of the National Anthem.

Capitals

NAME _____ SCORE _____

DIRECTIONS: There are words in each of the following sentences that should be capitalized. Write the correctly capitalized words in the blanks.

EXAMPLE

cynthia small was president of a   <u>Cynthia Small</u>
state college in california.   <u>California</u>

1. he told the team that he would return next   _____
   year, and said, "don't forget to study over   _____
   the summer."

2. "your president is not a crook" is a famous   _____
   statement from the watergate era.   _____

3. the declaration of independence was writ-   _____
   ten for all future americans, regardless of   _____
   race or religion.   _____

4. whether you are a christian, jew, or muslim,   _____
   or white, black or any other color, it's your   _____
   country.   _____
   _____

5. We can only be pulled apart by that old   _____
   devil, prejudice.

6. all who come here become americanized,   _____
   but can retain part of their native culture.   _____

7. Since she majored in the communication   _____
   field, she was able to find a job at fox-five.

8. George Pataki, the governor of New York state, is a republican.   _____

9. Every student of literature should read war and peace.   _____

10. Don't you wonder why thanksgiving is always on a Thursday?   _____

Capitals

NAME _____ SCORE _____

DIRECTIONS: The words listed here can be capitalized or not depending upon their use in respective sentences. Use each of the words in a sentence requiring its capitalization, and again in a sentence not requiring its capitalization. Consult your dictionary as necessary.

EXAMPLE

    Pride, pride   <u>His destruction was caused by Pride.</u>

                       <u>He takes pride in his work.</u>

1. President, president

_____

_____

2. Writer, writer

_____

_____

3. Army, army

_____

_____

4. Avenue, avenue

_____

_____

5. University, university

_____

_____

Chapter 24

Italics

To *italicize* means to emphasize; we emphasize certain aspects of our writing. As with capitalization, there are several rules to follow when italicizing. Consult a recently published dictionary for the most current standards. Underlining is an acceptable method of italicizing.

24a   Italics identify the titles of separate publications.

One of the best translations of "Oedipus Rex" is in *Sophocles—The Oedipus Cycle.*

In addition to newspapers, the titles of books, magazines, pamphlets, plays, and films are usually italicized. Italics also indicate the titles of television and radio programs, entire recordings, works of art, long poems, comic strips, genera (a class or group with common attributes), species, and software programs.

24b   Italics identify foreign words and phrases in the context of an English sentence.

If someone says *arigato* to you in Japan, you are being thanked.

24c   Italics identify the names of legal cases.

The People of the United States v. McVeigh

24d   Italics identify the names of specific ships, satellites, and spacecraft.

U.S.S. *New Jersey*

24e   Italics indicate words, letters, or figures spoken of as such or used as illustrations, statistical symbols, or the variables in algebraic expressions.

Remember, X marks the spot.

$C = \pi r^2$

24f   When used sparingly, italics indicate emphasis.

Everything was fine until *she* showed up.

Italics

NAME _____ SCORE _____

DIRECTIONS: In each of the following sentences, there are words and phrases that should be italicized. Rewrite the sentence making the necessary corrections. You may italicize by underlining.

EXAMPLE

Harrison Ford appeared in Star Wars.

Harrison Ford appeared in *Star Wars*.

1. Encarta has become a popular source for research papers.

   _____

2. There has been a lot of controversy over Roe v. Wade.

   _____

3. Bongiorno is a greeting commonly heard at the Columbus Day Parade.

   _____

4. It has been well over one million years since homo sapiens first walked
   the earth.

   _____

5. We did win that game.

   _____

6. The Apollo phase of the space program really put the United States in the
   forefront of the space program.

   _____

7. Pi is an essential symbol to know when studying geometry.

   _____

8. Did you see Kenneth Branaugh as Jago in Othello?

   _____

9. Spell Check is a good software program for writers, but be careful that the word itself is used appropriately.

_____

10. You had better study for that test.

_____

Italics Exercise 24–2

NAME _____ SCORE _____

DIRECTIONS: In the following sentences, underline the words and phrases that should be italicized.

1. Our public library doesn't subscribe to the Journal of Behavorial Science or to the Washington Post.

_____

_____

_____

2. Did you see today's Far Side strip in the New York Times?

_____

_____

3. I recently watched two documentaries: one about Brown v. the Board of Education and another about the sinking of the Titanic.

_____

_____

_____

4. Apparently, x = 35 was not the answer to the question.

_____

_____

5. I think Kenneth Branaugh's Hamlet is much better than the one starring Mel Gibson.

_____

_____

_____

6. The executive liked to refer to himself as homme d'affaires.

_____

_____

7. Do you prefer to type your papers in Word or WordPerfect?

_____

_____

8. When she was in New York City, she saw the Broadway hit Rent.

_____

_____

9. The new exhibit includes Munch's The Scream and Rodin's The Thinker.

_____

_____

10. We are required to read Milton's Paradise Lost and Jane Austen's Emma before the end of the semester.

_____

_____

Chapter 25

Abbreviations, Acronyms, and Numbers

(*Hodges* 11)   ab/ac/n 25

An abbreviation is a shortened form of a word, phrase, or any term we might use, chiefly in writing. An acronym is a word formed from the initial letters or parts of a word.

Abbreviations   Dr. (Doctor), TX (Texas)

Acronym   USMC (United States Marine Corps)

Currently accepted abbreviations can be found in a recently published dictionary.

25a   Designations such as *Ms., Mr., Mrs., Dr.*, and *St.* appear before a proper name, and those such as *Jr., Sr.*, and *II* appear after.

Dr. Jonas Salk; St. John's University
Edward Byrnes, Jr.; John Smith, III

25b   The names of states, countries, continents, months, days of the week, and units of measurement are not abbreviated when they appear in a sentence.

Last January, the Green Bay Packers, from Wisconsin, won the Super Bowl by beating the New England Patriots.

25c   Words such as *Street, Avenue, Road, Park*, and *Company* are abbreviated only when they appear in addresses.

Prospect Park is on Flatbush Avenue in Brooklyn, New York.

Prospect Park Zoo
Flatbush Ave.
Brooklyn, NY

25d The words *volume*, *chapter*, and *page* are usually written out when they appear in sentences but abbreviated when they appear in bibliographies and reference lists.

Shakespeare's first volume of poetry is 100 pages long in that edition.

Jan., January (and other months)
Coll., College

25e When unfamiliar with an acronym, readers benefit from seeing it spelled out the first time it is used.

The Police Athletic League is usually referred to as the PAL.

25f Numbers are written in different ways depending on the size of the numbers and the frequency with which they appear.

twenty-one; 121

When you use numbers infrequently in a piece of writing, you can spell out those that can be expressed in one or two words and use figures for the others. When you use numbers frequently, spell out those from one to nine and use figures for all others. Very large numbers can be expressed by a combination of words and figures.

one, two, three, twenty-one
247, 1,242
six million dollars; $6,000,000; or 6 million dollars

Abbreviations and Numbers   Exercise 25–1

NAME _____   SCORE _____

DIRECTIONS: Use your dictionary to look up the correct abbreviations for each underlined word in numbers 1–5. For numbers 6–10, convert the written numbers to standard Arabic numerals.

EXAMPLE

<u>Mister</u> Edward Jones, <u>Junior</u>   <u>Mr., Jr.</u>

One million four hundred thousand   <u>1,400,000</u>

1. Four hundred <u>pounds</u>   _____

2. <u>Montana</u>, near <u>Canada</u>   _____

3. <u>Mister</u> on the <u>mountain</u>   _____

4. <u>Broadway</u>, the wide <u>street</u>   _____

5. <u>Saint Paul</u>, <u>Minnesota</u>, in <u>April</u>   _____

6. Nineteen fifty-two   _____

7. Six and one-half million dollars   _____

8. Sixteen dollars and fifty-nine cents _____

9. The twenty-fifth of November,   _____
    nineteen ninety-seven

10. Fourteen twenty-two,   _____
    East Nineteenth Street

Abbreviations, Acronyms, and Numbers   Exercise 25–2

NAME _____ SCORE _____

DIRECTIONS: Rewrite the following sentences; applying the principles for abbreviations, acronyms, and numbers. (See *Harbrace* 25a through 25f; *Hodges* 11a through 11f.)

1. My mother will arrive at five o'clock in the afternoon.

    _____

2. After graduating, I hope to work at the National Aeronautics and Space Administration.

    _____

    _____

3. I spent twenty-five dollars and ten cents on a new sweater.

    _____

    _____

4. My father served in the United States Air Force after he graduated from high school in nineteen hundred sixty-five.

    _____

    _____

    _____

5. On the envelope, I used his home address: four thousand ninety Meadowlark Ave., Camp Hill, Pennsylvania seventeen thousand twelve.

    _____

    _____

6. Professor T.J. Williams, Junior enjoys writing screenplays.

    _____

    _____

7. Our class reunion will be held on November sixteen, nineteen hundred ninety-eight.

    _____

    _____

8. My best friend attends Saint Mary's University in San Antonio, Texas.

   _____

   _____

9. Mister Taylor often watches the National Football League games on television.

   _____

   _____

10. I read pages thirty-seven to forty-two of chapter four in volume two of the abnormal psychology series.

    _____

    _____

Review: Capitals, Italics, Abbreviations, Numbers

NAME _____ SCORE _____

DIRECTIONS: Rewrite the following paragraph. Capitalize, italicize, and abbreviate whenever appropriate. Write the correct number designation wherever necessary.

EXAMPLE

john went to new york to see the central park production of hamlet. it began at 8.

   John went to New York to see the Central Park production of *Hamlet.*

   It began at 8:00 p.m.

[1]When Marie went to her first english class in college she was assigned the red badge of courage, a novel about the civil war written by stephen crane in the late 19 century. [2]she thought doctor smith, her professor, would discuss the novel first, then test them. [3]at ten the next morning dr smith gave the class a quiz. [4]marie wasn't prepared, so she received a 55, which is a failing grade.

_____

_____

_____

_____

_____

_____

_____

_____

_____

_____

_____

_____

_____

Chapter 26

Document Design

(Hodges 8)   des 26

You are about to begin the chapters in this book covering paragraphs and the essay. Before you begin extended writing, however, it is important to consider format, neatness, and consistency of presentation. Your instructor may wish to assign a particular style and form for you to follow when presenting papers. The suggestions that follow are generally acceptable, but not unique. They are guidelines that your instructor may choose to change or ignore. The point, however, is that you discipline yourself to work on the presentation as well as the content of your papers. As you progress in your writing at the college level, you will be exposed to styles for presenting research papers, technical papers, and so on. For now, concentrate on making your presentation neat and readable.

26a   Using the proper materials enhances readability.

Normally, you should write on 8 1/2-by-11-inch white paper. It should be unlined for typed papers, or papers done on a computerized printer, and lined for handwritten papers, as you will be doing in class. Put your papers together with a paper clip or staple; never fold them unless instructed to do so. Do not use folders unless instructed to. Follow your instructor's directions regarding work done on a disk or other electronic means. *Always* ask for clarification. Don't do work based on the assumption that it's all right if you aren't certain it's all right.

26b   Clear and orderly arrangement contributes to ease in reading.

Follow your instructor's directions about margins, type, font size, and so on. If he or she doesn't give you instructions, ask for them.

26c   The appropriate form for electronic documents can vary.

Most of your papers as a beginning writer will be done by hand, and probably in class. Should you get to the stage where you are producing electronic documents, ask for specific instructions. *Never* assume you can "do your own thing," and forget the attitude of "whatever."

26d   Proofreading provides quality control.

When you **revise**, you might change or reorganize your paper. When you **edit**, you clarify the structure of your paper. **Proofreading** checks for errors in structure, grammar, layout, mechanics, and so on. Make certain you proofread carefully before handing in a paper, whether it's a paper you've done at home with plenty of time for completion, or a paper done in class with time constraints. Budget your time so that you will be able to proofread.

Establish a Checklist

NAME _____ SCORE _____

DIRECTIONS: Establish a checklist that you can use before handing in papers. The list should include checks for proper materials, margins, pagination, structure and content of the assignment, proper length, and legibility if handwritten. Use this checklist whenever you write a paper. Revise it as you progress and become more familiar with writing papers.

Chapter 27

Working with Paragraphs

(Hodges 31)   ¶ 27

Learning to construct good paragraphs is an essential step toward writing good essays. The paragraph can be thought of as a mini-essay, in that it follows a similar development process: main idea (topic sentence), supporting ideas (supporting sentences). When we add transitional devices to the paragraph, we establish a flow of ideas and a sense of unity in the essay. In fact, the concepts of unity and coherence that we implemented when studying sentences apply to paragraphs, only on a larger scale. Your paragraphs, then, should be **unified, coherent,** and **well developed.**

The length of your paragraphs will probably vary within a range of 50 to 150 words. A paragraph that is only one sentence long, or only 50 words long and comprised of short, choppy sentences, shows a lack of development. A paragraph that is 200 words long, or longer, or an essay that is all one paragraph, all show a lack of organization.

27a Paragraphs should be unified.

There should be one topic sentence, or main idea, in each paragraph. The other sentences in the paragraph should support and relate to the topic sentence. The topic sentence may be placed at the beginning of the paragraph, announcing your main idea immediately. It can be placed in the middle of the paragraph so that you can put your supporting and transitional sentences around it. It can be placed at the end of the paragraph so that you present evidence, as it were, and lead the reader to a conclusion, which is your main idea. Consider, in some instances, placing your topic sentence at the beginning of the paragraph and restating it at the end, using either the same words or the same idea stated differently; this gives emphasis to the main idea.

Topic sentence

Jose wants to make his college experience the most important part of his life. He saved his money to pay for application fees, wrote to college

Supporting examples and details

admissions offices for applications, and scheduled appointments to visit several colleges. All of this was done early in his senior year of high school, when it should be done. His parents remarked how this is the most organized he has ever been in his

Idea repeated for emphasis (also reinforces main idea)

life. Jose must be serious about placing importance on his college career.

Jose must be serious about the importance of college in his life. He saved his money to pay for application fees, wrote to college admission offices for applications, and even scheduled appointments to visit several colleges. Jose wants to make his

Topic sentence in body paragraph

college experience the most important part of his life. He did all this in his senior year, when it should be done. His parents even remarked how this is the most organized he has been in his entire life.

Jose must be serious about placing importance on his college career. Even his parents have remarked how this is the most organized he's been in his entire life. He saved money to pay for application fees, wrote to college admission offices for applications, and scheduled appointments to visit several colleges. All of this was done in his senior year, when it should be done. Obviously, Jose wants to

Topic sentence at end

make his college experience the most important part of his life.

27b   Clearly arranged ideas and effective transitions foster paragraph coherence.

Your subject should be clear to the reader throughout your paragraph (and essay). In order to do this, you must arrange your ideas in some clearly understandable order. Keep your sentences in chronological order (the sequence of events shouldn't jump around in time), and spatial order (don't jump from place to place; keep logical order to the movements you describe in your writing). Move from general to specific, as in the third paragraph presented in 27a, or specific to general, as in the first paragraph. Use transitional devices such as pronouns, repetition, transitional words and phrases, and parallel structures to move your reader smoothly and logically from idea to idea, sentence to sentence, paragraph to paragraph.

Pronoun transition	*Jose* wants to make his college experience the most important part of *his* life. *He* saved his money....
Repetition of words, phrases, or ideas	saved, wrote, scheduled [verbs connote mature activities] opening and closing sentences of paragraph
Parallel structure	Above repeats the same idea, linking the paragraph one end to the other. He saved . . . to pay, wrote . . . for applications, scheduled . . . to visit [subject, verb—phrase]

Transitions between paragraphs are as important as transitions within each paragraph. Your written ideas must flow from paragraph to paragraph, and your reader should not be jolted from idea to idea. The following chart lists some frequently used transitional connections arranged according to the kinds of relationships they establish.

CHECKLIST OF TRANSITIONAL CONNECTIONS

Alternative and addition	or, not, and, and then, moreover, besides, further, furthermore, likewise, also, too, again, in addition, even more important, next, first, second, third, in the first place, in the second place, finally, last
Comparison	similarly, likewise, in like manner
Contrast	but, yet, or, and yet, however, still, nevertheless, on the other hand, on the contrary, conversely, even so, notwithstanding, in contrast, at the same time, although this may be true, otherwise, nonetheless
Place	here, beyond, nearby, opposite to, adjacent to, on the opposite side, to this end, for this purpose, with this object
Result or cause	so, for, therefore, accordingly, consequently, thus, thereupon, as a result, then, because, hence
Summary	to sum up, in brief, on the whole, in sum, in short
Repetition	as I have said, in other words, that is, to be sure, as has been noted
Exemplification	for example, for instance, in any event

Intensification	in fact, indeed, to tell the truth
Time	meanwhile, at length, soon, after a few days, in the meantime, afterward, after, now, then, in the past, while

Not all the preceding connectors would be appropriate as paragraph-to-paragraph transitions, but many can be used, depending on the situation.

Topic sentence at end of paragraph 3 above	Obviously, Jose wants to make his college experience the most important of his life.
Transition to new paragraph	To this end, he has organized his habits and his lifestyle to accommodate his goals.

27c   Details and examples can develop paragraphs.

Your topic sentence needs information added to it for the purposes of demonstration, support, and proof. Although it's your main idea, your reader wants and needs more information to better understand what idea you are trying to convey. Notice in the paragraphs presented in 27a that no matter where the topic sentence is placed, the details and examples of Jose's behavior are all closely related to his goal of making college important.

27d Writers use various strategies to develop paragraphs.

Whenever you read a newspaper, essay, work of fiction, or textbook, notice the author uses various techniques to present the paragraphs and the entire work. These techniques include comparison and contrast, process analysis, classification, cause and effect, and definition. These are all **expository techniques** that you will be using in your writing once you have mastered the basics of writing. Your instructor may introduce you to one or more of those techniques after you have had practice writing narratives (relating an incident or telling a story) and descriptions (describing an experience, an event, or a person or thing).

27e Editing can improve paragraph logic and effectiveness.

Revising and editing can occur at any time during your writing. A convenient and sensible time might be after each paragraph is finished. Check the paragraph for logic, clarity, structure, but also remember unity, coherence, and development. Go over the entire essay each time you edit a paragraph, and be certain that each paragraph fits into the essay. Make necessary changes at any time before the final draft is written.

CHECKLIST FOR REVISING PARAGRAPHS

- Do all the ideas in the paragraph belong?
- Are any necessary ideas left out?
- Is the paragraph coherent? Do the sentences focus on the topic? Do they link to previous sentences? Is the order of sentences logical?
- Are sentences connected to each other with easy, effective, and natural transitions? Is the paragraph linked to the preceding and following paragraphs?
- Is the paragraph adequately developed? If there are problems, can analyzing the strategy used to develop the paragraphs help solve the problem?

Paragraph Unity

Exercise 27–1

NAME _____ SCORE _____

DIRECTIONS: For each of the following subjects, write a topic sentence that you would use if you were writing a paragraph on that subject. Choose three of the sentences you have written, and use them as the topic sentences for three-to-five-sentence paragraphs. Write one paragraph with the topic sentence at the beginning, one with the topic sentence in the body of the paragraph, and one with the topic sentence at the end. Underline the topic sentence in each paragraph.

1. Should college athletes have a special grading system?

   _____

   _____

2. We should stop space exploration and use the money at home.

   _____

   _____

3. Reinstitute the draft.

   _____

   _____

4. Religious displays should/should not be permitted on public property.

   _____

   _____

5. Allow/Don't allow tax credits for families that send their children to parochial schools.

   _____

   _____

_____

_____

_____

_____

_____

_____

_____

_____

_____

_____

_____

_____

_____

_____

_____

_____

_____

_____

_____

_____

_____

_____

_____

_____

_____

Effective Transitions and Coherence   Exercise 27–2

NAME _____ SCORE _____

DIRECTIONS: Following are the first and last sentences for three paragraphs. Develop the middle of each paragraph with three to five sentences, using proper transitional devices and techniques to produce coherent paragraphs. Underline the topic sentence in each paragraph.

1. Research has shown that a significant number of women want to play on co-ed teams.

_____

_____

_____

_____

_____

_____

_____

Women should not be prevented from playing any sport for which they can qualify.

2. When I first began attending college, I had no idea what I wanted to do with my life.

_____

_____

_____

_____

_____

_____

_____

One year can certainly make a lot of difference in terms of a young man's/woman's career plans.

3. There is no single method of solving the graffiti problem.

_____

_____

_____

_____

_____

_____

_____

_____

_____

By using this combination of techniques, graffiti could at least be mini-
mized, if not stopped altogether.

Details and Examples

Exercise 27–3

NAME _____ SCORE _____

DIRECTIONS: For each of the topic sentences you wrote in Exercise 27–1, make a list of at least five details or examples you could use if you were writing a paragraph with that sentence as the topic sentence. Rewrite the sentences, and write the five or more items beneath each sentence.

1. _____

_____

_____

_____

_____

_____

_____

2. _____

_____

_____

_____

_____

_____

_____

3. _____

_____

_____

_____

_____

_____

_____

4. _____

_____

_____

_____

_____

_____

_____

5. _____

_____

_____

_____

_____

_____

_____

Harcourt Brace & Company

Chapter 28

Planning and Drafting Essays

(Hodges 32)   pln/dft 28

When you are assigned a topic on which you must write an essay, a process begins. The process is made up of steps, beginning with planning and ending with the submission of the assignment to your instructor. Much occurs between those two phases.

Many students, especially those who are new to writing in college, try to sit down, pen-in-hand, and write a paper of the assigned length by just blurting out on paper what they think is a unified, cohesive, well-developed essay. One of two things will probably occur: you experience "writer's block," where nothing happens and you sit there looking at the blank paper, unable to "create"; or, just as likely, you fill up a page or two with poorly formed paragraphs, lines of irrelevant material, and no proper development of ideas. Remember, you cannot plan and organize *as* you write—those two steps, planning and organizing, must be done *before* you write.

Once the planning stage is complete, write a draft of your essay. The draft is a work copy for you to edit and revise before writing the final copy. Changes and corrections are made on the draft copy. If you don't plan and draft, you diminish your chances dramatically of handing in a good paper that will get a good grade.

28a   Writers must understand their purpose, audience, and occasion.

The **purpose** of your writing means the reason why you're writing it. The obvious but shallow responses are "for a good grade" or "because it is assigned." Your real purpose should include the desire to learn how to write better while completing an assignment that you should consider a challenge as well as an obligation. The purpose of your assignment could be to express how you feel about something, to explain something, or to persuade someone (that is, your audience) to adopt a point of view or undertake a course of action.

The **audience** is who will read your writing. This will usually consist of your instructor and, on occasion, your classmates. Now you have a purpose that must be adapted to your audience. An important consideration at this point is the appropriateness of your presentation to your particular audience. Your instructor may vary the assignment and tell you to direct your writing to a specific audience, such as a government agency or an environmental protection group.

The **occasion** means the circumstances under which writers and readers communicate. The writer must adjust style, tone, and level of diction to the audience, keeping in mind the specific circumstances under which the writing is done. For example, if an assignment in history is to write an analysis of the Holocaust, humor would be in poor taste. A somber, heavy tone would not fit in a paper about a family reunion during the holidays. In another sense, occasion could mean the actual occasion of the writing. It could be an initial placement essay, a first assignment, or a final assignment that decides whether or not you pass or fail. Each occasion is different, and each of your approaches to the respective papers should be different.

28b Writers need to find appropriate subjects.

In most instances, your instructor will assign the topic you will write on. On occasion, you will be able to choose your own topic, or the assigned topic will be so broad as to require extensive narrowing down. In either situation, you must choose and restrict, or just restrict, the topic so that it can be handled within the parameters of your assignment (length, number of words, pages, etc.). For example, you might be assigned to write a paper on a personal experience, or a paper on any subject you feel comfortable with. In either situation, describing a personal experience that changed your life focuses on an aspect of your experience that can be described quite well in a short (300–400 word) essay. The key is to restrict your topic and focus on an aspect of the topic that (1) meets the requirements of the assignment, (2) lends itself well to your audience's tastes, and (3) can be dealt with in an organized manner that isn't too vague or general.

28c By exploring subjects you can focus on a topic.

Writers on all levels frequently keep journals. In the journals, instead of writing about events, write feelings and analyses about the events. For instance, if you observe someone feeding pigeons in a park, instead of merely stating the fact, you could describe the person, the park, the pigeons, and attempt to capture the human aspect of the situation. That could be the subject of a human interest paper or a paper that describes a significant incident.

Freewriting is a technique that could be used to find a subject or to write a draft (see 28f). Get your pencil and paper in front of you, set a time limit (10 or 15 minutes), and write whatever occurs to you without stopping. If you need a subject and you're truly freewriting, one or more will surface. If you have a subject and you freewrite on that subject, you'll be amazed at how much pertinent information you will put on the paper. This information has to be organized, but that's easily done by outlining (see 28e).

Other methods of gathering information from your own experiences include **listing**, where you make an informal list of ideas pertaining to the subject, and **questioning**, where you ask yourself *Who? What? Where? When?* and *How?* about the subject. Try each of the focusing methods or a combination of them, and use the one or ones you are comfortable with as long as it is the method from which you get the best results. Once you find that method, stick with it.

28d   A clearly stated thesis conveys your main idea.

Beginning writers are better served by making a thesis statement instead of implying one or requiring the reader to figure out what it is. The clearly stated thesis serves as a guide as well as a safety device for the writer. It keeps you on course and gives you a reference point to refer to constantly so that the essay does not wander or violate any rules of unity or coherence. Assume you're assigned to write an essay about your senior year in high school. How focused should your thesis statement be?

Vague   My senior year was busy.

Focused   During my senior year in high school, I studied for the SATs, applied to and visited several colleges, and kept a part-time job.

The focused statement is easier for the reader to understand and for the writer to follow in the essay. It serves as a guide to the organization of the essay.

28e   Arranging ideas requires choosing an appropriate method or combination of methods.

You have chosen and restricted a topic, focused on the topic and accumulated information about it, and formulated a thesis. The next step in writing your paper is to arrange and organize your ideas. Some type of outline should be made. It can be informal or structured, but become accustomed to making detailed, comprehensive outlines for the papers you write at home, and practice making short but well-organized outlines for the papers or exams you write in class. Once you establish a planning technique that suits you and works well for you, use it before each writing.

Informal plan   Thesis: During my senior year in high school, I was too busy to play football.
1. Study for SATs.
2. Apply to colleges; visit colleges.
3. Work part time job for college tuition.
4. Take standardized tests besides SATs.
5. Attend College Nights with parents.

This list can be reorganized; 1 and 4, 2 and 5 can be combined, and three major ideas can be developed into paragraphs.

Formal topic outline

Thesis: During my senior year in high school, I was too busy to play football.

I. Studying for standardized tests
    A. SATs, state tests
        1. College placement tests
        2. English and math review
    B. Special course for SAT score enhancement
        1. Travel to school for classes
        2. Practice tests on own time
        3. Budget time to study for regular courses
II. College applications
    A. Attend College Nights with parents
        1. Another night out
        2. Go to unfamiliar high schools
        3. Listen to college representatives
    B. Visit colleges
        1. Drive all over this and other states
        2. Gauge comfort level at each school
        3. Talk to students at each college
    C. Fill out and send in applications
        1. Expenses—work extra hours for application fees
        2. Write essay with each application
III. Work to earn money for college
    A. Supplement parents' expenses
    B. Money for expensive application fees
    C. Hidden expenses hurt parents' budget
IV. Football can wait
    A. Set priorities
        1. Education first
        2. Work second
        3. Football third
    B. Satisfy football cravings watching games on television

As you can see, the detailed topic outline is the framework for your essay. Each main heading (roman numerals) can be expanded into a topic sentence, so I, II, III, and IV are the bases for paragraphs. All the letters and numbers can be expanded to become supporting sentences. Provide transitions, and you have your essay. Once you become adept at making outlines, you'll find that you will be able to revise and reorganize the outline itself, instead of extensively changing your draft. The entries in a topic outline can be written in sentence form (sentence outline).

28f   Your first draft will not be your final draft.

If you plan and organize well, that is, if you learn to outline well, your first draft will require a minimum of revision. Usually, it will be your introduction, transitions, and conclusion that will need revision. Revise those areas, and write your second draft. This should be close to your finished product.

28g   Studying a first draft helps writers to see how it can be improved.

Reading a draft aloud will tell you a lot about your paper. You become, in a sense, your own audience. If it doesn't sound just right, you probably need to revise some more.

Exploring and Focusing   Exercise 28–1

NAME _____ SCORE _____

DIRECTIONS: Using a combination of journals, freewriting, and listing, explore the topics shown here to the point where you feel you have enough information to formulate a thesis on each topic.

1. Freedom of the press versus First Amendment rights.

_____

_____

_____

_____

_____

_____

_____

_____

_____

2. Whose responsibility is it to care for the homeless?

_____

_____

_____

_____

_____

_____

_____

_____

_____

_____

3. Reinstitution of the draft.

_____

_____

_____

_____

_____

_____

_____

_____

_____

4. Cloning human beings.

_____

_____

_____

_____

_____

_____

_____

_____

_____

Harcourt Brace & Company

Thesis Statements and Outlines   Exercise 28–2

NAME _____   SCORE _____

DIRECTIONS: Using the information you accumulated for each topic in Exercise 28–1, write a clear, focused thesis statement for each of those topics, and develop a topic outline for each of them.

1. _____

   _____

   _____

   _____

   _____

   _____

   _____

   _____

   _____

   _____

   _____

   _____

2. _____

   _____

   _____

   _____

   _____

   _____

   _____

   _____

   _____

   _____

   _____

   _____

3. _____

_____

_____

_____

_____

_____

_____

_____

_____

_____

_____

_____

_____

4. _____

_____

_____

_____

_____

_____

_____

_____

_____

_____

_____

_____

_____

Harcourt Brace & Company

Drafting and Revising

NAME _____ SCORE _____

DIRECTIONS: Choose one of the topics developed in Exercises 28–1 and 28–2 and write a draft for a 300–350 word essay. When the draft is finished, write an alternative introduction and conclusion. Underline all transitional devices (words, phrases, etc.) you use to link paragraphs.

_____

_____

_____

_____

_____

_____

_____

_____

_____

_____

_____

_____

_____

_____

_____

_____

_____

_____

_____

_____

_____

_____

_____

_____

Chapter 29

Revising and Editing Essays

(*Hodges* 33)   rev/ed 29

When we **revise**, we change or modify what we've written. When we **edit**, we make our writing more suitable for presentation. Revising deals with the ideas, content, and organization of writing, whereas editing deals more with mechanics: sentence structure, spelling, and so on.

29a Your tone reveals your attitude.

Our **tone** is the way we express something. The way we choose, arrange, and punctuate our words tells our audience how we feel about something. In other words, the tone we use in our writing, as in a spoken tone of voice, lets the reader know our attitude concerning the subject we're writing about. That means we must be careful that our tone is appropriate for the assignment and the audience. Let's suppose you're writing a paper on the revisions of the welfare system. You could say, "Revisions in the system have resulted in many deserving recipients being left without financial assistance." Or you could also say, "The long-needed revisions have helped eliminate fraud and taken plenty of freeloaders out of the system." In each of these statements, the writer's tone reveals clearly what he or she thinks of welfare. The first is concerned and compassionate, the second cold and short-sighted.

29b Revision is essential to writing well.

Anytime you change the organization of your writing or adjust the direction of an argument, you are revising. Revising is a healthy process because we are improving the presentation of our ideas for the audience's benefit. It is probably a good procedure to finish your draft before revising so that you can see how your own ideas flow and come together. Revising as you go along could result in choppy sentences and ideas with faulty transitions, especially between paragraphs.

29c Editing improves your writing.

Once you have revised your draft and are satisfied with the content of your essay, it is time to edit. Check your sentences for unity, variety, parallel structure, agreement, emphasis—all those areas covered in chapters 8 through 16. Also check diction, spelling, and punctuation—in other words, structure and mechanics.

Checklist for Editing

Sentences
- Are ideas related effectively through subordination and coordination (9)?
- Are all sentences united (8)?
- Do any sentences contain misplaced parts or dangling modifiers (5)?
- Is there any faulty parallelism (10)?
- Are there any needless shifts in grammatical structures, in tone or style, or in viewpoint (8e)?
- Are ideas given appropriate emphasis within each sentence (11)?
- Are the sentences varied in length and in type (12)?
- Are there any fragments (2)? Are there any comma splices or fused sentences (3)?
- Do all verbs agree with their subjects (7a)? Do all pronouns agree with their antecedents (6a)?
- Are all verb forms appropriate (7)?

Diction
- Are any words overused, imprecise, or vague (14, 14a)? Are all words idiomatic (14b)?
- Have all unnecessary words and phrases been eliminated (15)? Have any necessary words been left out by mistake (16)?
- Is the vocabulary appropriate for the audience, purpose, and occasion (13, 28a)?
- Have all technical words that might be unfamiliar to the audience been eliminated or defined (13c)?

Punctuation and mechanics
- Is all punctuation correct (17, 18, 19, 20, 21)? Are any marks missing?
- Are all words spelled correctly (22)?
- Is capitalization correct (23)?
- Are titles identified by either quotation marks (20c) or italics (24a)?
- Are abbreviations appropriate and correct (25)?

29d Proofreading can help make your papers error-free.

After you have completed revising and editing, make a final, thorough search to try to make the paper error-free. Write your final, ready-to-hand-in copy according to your instructor's directions (see Chapter 28). Part of your final proofread should include making certain the paper is done *exactly* as prescribed, *not* the way you want to do it. Don't think, "Professor Smith will like it better this way." Professor Smith won't.

29e You can benefit from studying how other writers work.

A good way to revise and proofread is to do it with a classmate. Frequently, instructors in college writing courses will divide the class into groups of three or four students. Each group shares information within the group and, occasionally, with other groups, during a freewriting session (see 28c). Each group also exchanges drafts within the group, and some creative revising, editing, and proofreading can occur. Each member of a group benefits from having his or her paper read by two or three classmates, and each member gets to read two or three papers with the different ideas in them. It also sharpens your critical and editing skills if you are not personally involved in reading your own paper.

29f The final draft reflects the care the writer took.

Take pride in having completed the process of planning, drafting, revising, editing, proofreading, and handing in an essay of high quality. As your level of writing sophistication increases, all the work entailed in early writing becomes habitual, and you will be producing longer, more complicated, and better papers.

Revising and Editing Essays

Exercise 29–1

NAME _____ SCORE _____

DIRECTIONS: (1) Select a piece of your writing, preferably an essay from one of your college or high school courses, and revise the essay making any necessary developmental changes and using the Checklist for Editing to further refine the coherence and style. (2) Once you have finished editing the essay, consider how the process of revision compares to the process of writing a first draft; write a short description, at least a paragraph, of the similarities and differences between these two processes. Be prepared to turn in the original and revised copies of your essay as well as your comparison of the drafting and revision processes.

_____

_____

_____

_____

_____

_____

_____

_____

_____

_____

_____

_____

_____

_____

_____

_____

_____

_____

_____

Answers to Odd-Numbered Exercises

CHAPTER 1

Exercise 1–1 *(Harbrace 1a, 1b; Hodges 1a, 1b)*

1. <u>she</u>, <u>was</u>, <u>member</u>

3. <u>time</u>, <u>was</u>, <u>scarce</u>

5. <u>she</u> <u>slept</u>; (<u>she</u>) <u>woke</u> (up)

7. <u>she</u>, <u>plans</u>

(Harbrace 1a; Hodges 1a)

Verbs with prepositions	*Verbs with auxiliaries*
5. woke up	7. will

Exercise 1–2 *(Harbrace 1a, 1b; Hodges 1a, 1b)*

1. Marie, Mark, will graduate	5. You, don't wait
3. They, are preparing	7. Mark, wants

(Harbrace 1b; Hodges 1b)

1. noun, compound	5. pronoun, singular
3. pronoun, plural	7. noun, singular

Exercise 1–3 *(Harbrace 1a, 1b; Hodges 1a, 1b)*

1. <u>Marcia</u>, <u>John</u>, <u>will go</u>

3. <u>Marcia</u>, <u>became</u>, <u>book-buyer</u>

5. <u>both</u>, <u>seem</u>, <u>anxious</u>

7. <u>list</u>, <u>was</u>, <u>longer</u>; <u>Engineering Department</u>, <u>requires</u>, <u>literature</u>, <u>history</u>

(Harbrace 1b; Hodges 1b)

1. (none)
3. book-buyer (do)

5. anxious (sc)
7. longer (sc); literature, history (do)

Exercise 1–4
Answers may vary.

Exercise 1–5
Answers may vary.

Exercise 1–6 *(Harbrace 1d; Hodges 1d)*
The following phrases should be underlined:

[1]At their high school graduation ceremony
[3]about their driving carefully, in his car, to make sure

1. At their high school graduation ceremony; *prepositional phrase*
3. about their driving carefully, in his car; *prepositional phrases*

Exercise 1–7 *(Harbrace 1e; Hodges 1e)*
Answers may vary; here is one possible reorganization.

[1]John and Maria, <u>having graduated in June</u>, finished high school. [2]They will start college next fall. [3]John will major in humanities <u>because he wants to be a teacher</u>. [4]Maria, <u>since she wants to be a doctor</u>, will major in biology. [5]<u>When they leave home in September</u>, they will both go to the same state college. [6]<u>That John and Maria haven't lived away from home before</u> makes it more exciting for them. [7]<u>Since it's such an important part of their lives</u>, they can't wait until September <u>when their parents drive them</u>.

Exercise 1–8 *(Harbrace 1f; Hodges 1f)*

1. simple, imperative
3. compound, declarative
5. complex, declarative
7. compound, imperative
9. compound, declarative

Harcourt Brace & Company

CHAPTER 2

Exercise 2–1 (*Harbrace* 2a; *Hodges* 2a)

1. v, verb
3. p, subj/verb
5. p, subj/verb
7. p, subj/verb
9. a, subj/verb
11. v, verb
13. a, subj/verb
15. sp, subj

Exercise 2–2 (*Harbrace* 2b; *Hodges* 2b)
Answers may vary. The following are possible corrections.

1. She took a taxi because it was late at night.
3. John studied all night, even though he was tired.
5. Because Marie's grades, which were better than John's, however, enabled her to go to the party.
7. Between studying and working, there will be little free time for socializing.
9. Call someone in your class in regard to Friday's English test.

CHAPTER 3

Exercise 3–1 (*Harbrace* 3a, 3b; *Hodges* 3a, 3b)

1. cs, A or D
3. cs, B or C
5. f, D
7. c
9. cs, f; A and D

Exercise 3–2 (*Harbrace* 3; *Hodges* 3)
Answers may vary.

1. I needed help revising my conclusion, so my peer tutor helped me refocus it.
3. I suddenly remembered that my class would meet in the library; consequently, I quickly picked up my books and left the classroom.
5. We had two hours to finish the test; I finished in one hour.
7. My roommate eats her lunch in our dormitory room, but I usually eat in the cafeteria with friends.
9. His friends went to the football game; however, he couldn't go with them because he had to study.

Review: Comma Splices, Fused Sentences, Fragments (*Harbrace* 2, 3; *Hodges* 2, 3)

1. Now that you have become accustomed to writing grammatically correct sentences, it shouldn't be difficult to develop good paragraphs; they come naturally once sentence structure is mastered.
3. Writing sentences correctly then becomes second nature.
5. After you graduate, you'll appreciate the ability to write well, especially later when you apply for a job.

CHAPTER 4

Exercise 4–1

1. perfect, adj.	(*Harbrace* 4c; *Hodges* 4c)
3. best, adj.	(*Harbrace* 4c; *Hodges* 4c)
5. better, adv.	(*Harbrace* 4c, *Hodges* 4c)
7. certainly, adv.	(*Harbrace* 4a; *Hodges* 4a)
careful, adj.	(*Harbrace* 4b; *Hodges* 4b)
9. higher, adj.	(*Harbrace* 4b, 4c; *Hodges* 4b, 4c)
11. difficult, adj.	(*Harbrace* 4b; *Hodges* 4b)
13. no, adj.	(*Harbrace* 4c; *Hodges* 4c)
15. lucky, adj.	(*Harbrace* 4b; *Hodges* 4b)
happy, adj.	(*Harbrace* 4b; *Hodges* 4b)
careful, adj.	(*Harbrace* 4b; *Hodges* 4b)

Exercise 4–2 (*Harbrace* 4c, 4; *Hodges* 4c, 4)

1. newer, newest, newly
3. littler, littlest, less (or least)
5. slower, slowest, slowly
7. worse, worst, worse
9. better, best, well

CHAPTER 5

Exercise 5–1 (*Harbrace* 5a; *Hodges* 25a)

1. John almost finished his lunch.   <u>finished</u>

3. Ed went to class the next day.   <u>went</u>

5. At her desk, Marie wrote a letter about her schedule.   <u>wrote</u>

7. They nearly all agreed that college was not
like high school.   <u>all</u>

Or They all nearly agreed that college was not
like high school.   <u>agreed</u>

Or They all agreed that college was not nearly
like high school.   <u>was</u>

9. The test that they would take on Monday would
be difficult.   <u>test</u>

Exercise 5–2 (*Harbrace* 5b; *Hodges* 25b)

1. Dinner was delayed because Marie's mother remembered that she was still at
school.
3. The car was at the far end of the parking lot, so we had to walk a while
before finding it.
5. In order to get good grades, one must study from good notes.

CHAPTER 6

Exercise 6–1

1. mine, *or* his, *or* hers	(*Harbrace* 6, introduction; *Hodges* 5, introduction)
3. them, they	(*Harbrace* 6a; *Hodges* 6b)
5. I	(*Harbrace* 6c; *Hodges* 5a)
7. his	(*Harbrace* 6, introduction; *Hodges* 5, introduction)
9. who	(*Harbrace* 6b; *Hodges* 28)
11. myself	(*Harbrace* 6, introduction; *Hodges* 5, introduction)
13. whom	(*Harbrace* 6d; *Hodges* 5c)
15. whose	(*Harbrace* 6, introduction; *Hodges* 5, introduction)

Exercise 6–2 (*Harbrace* 6a; *Hodges* 6b)

1. <u>John</u>, me

3. <u>John</u>, who

5. <u>teacher</u>, his *or* her

7. <u>Telling</u>, them

9. <u>You</u>, me

CHAPTER 7

Exercise 7–1 (*Harbrace* 7b, introduction; *Hodges* 7a, introduction)

1. write, wrote, written; I, tr
3. bring, brought, brought; I, tr
5. learn, learned, learned; R, tr
7. hide, hid, hid; I, tr
9. see, saw, seen; I, tr
11. wind, wound, wound; I, tr
13. take, took, taken; I, tr
15. creep, crept, crept; I, in

Exercise 7–2

1. understood, meant	(*Harbrace* 7c; *Hodges* 7c)
3. will pass, studies	(*Harbrace* 7c; *Hodges* 7c)
5. worked, failed	(*Harbrace* 7e; *Hodges* 7e)
7. will be needing	(*Harbrace* 7c; *Hodges* 7c)
9. are	(*Harbrace* 7a; *Hodges* 6a)
11. is	(*Harbrace* 7a; *Hodges* 6a)
13. is	(*Harbrace* 7a; *Hodges* 6a)
15. won't regret, having studied, get	(*Harbrace* 7c; *Hodges* 7c)

Review: Coherence, Pronouns, Verbs
Answers may vary. Here is one possible method of rewriting the paragraph.

1. After having gone to orientation, which was long, Marie and Joe moved into dormitories, which were far apart and a long walk from each other.
3. It was closed, so they went back to their rooms hungry and did some studying.
5. The college had its first welcoming party.

CHAPTER 8

Exercise 8–1
Answers may vary.

1. Marie moved into her dormitory on her first day at college. Even though it was raining, she enjoyed looking at the lovely campus. (*Harbrace* 8b; *Hodges* 23b)
3. The holidays are a good time to go to the theater or movies to see a Shakespearean play. The modernized versions are easier to understand. (*Harbrace* 8a; *Hodges* 23a)
5. If you live in the city, you can go to a college near home and stay with your family. Public transportation is inexpensive, and you won't have to pay for room and board. (*Harbrace* 8b; *Hodges* 23b)

Exercise 8–2

1. Marie's paper was good, but she didn't hand it in on time. <u>Mix</u> (*Harbrace* 8c; *Hodges* 23c)
3. Fred was still wrong, and his friends told him if he didn't change his approach he'd end up in deep water (*or* hot water). <u>Mix</u> (*Harbrace* 8c; *Hodges* 23c)
5. Marie went to class, and Juan went to the movies. <u>Shift</u> (*Harbrace* 8e; *Hodges* 23e)

CHAPTER 9

Exercise 9–1 (*Harbrace* 9a; *Hodges* 24a)
Answers may vary.

1. Cindy is going to go to an inexpensive state college near her home. She'll save money that can be used later for graduate school. It's also convenient to drive to school.
3. Next you will take either American, British, or World Literature, all of which are interesting, but be prepared to read a lot.
5. Whether you're going to a public or private college, living at home or away, it's important to develop good study habits in high school so you can try to get scholarship money, which helps.

Exercise 9–2

Answers may vary.

1. Since Ed got the highest science grades in high school, half his tuition is scholarship money. (*Harbrace* 9c; *Hodges* 24c)
3. On the day the home team lost the big game, John's car broke down. (*Harbrace* 9b; *Hodges* 24b)
5. John has five courses, plays baseball, and wants to get a part-time job because he needs spending money, but he won't be able to do all those things and study as much as he needs to. (*Harbrace* 9b; *Hodges* 24b)

CHAPTER 10

Exercise 10–1

1. that would be, that would be, that would (*Harbrace* 10a; *Hodges* 26a)
3. in the achievement, in the knowledge, in the ability (*Harbrace* 10b; *Hodges* 26b)
5. running, swimming, dieting (*Harbrace* 10a; *Hodges* 26a)

Exercise 10–2

1. College tuition is paid by student and public money. (*Harbrace* 10a; *Hodges* 26a)
3. He told me that he was going to work and that I should too. (*Harbrace* 10a; *Hodges* 26a)
5. John thought it would be a good idea if we all worked together, if we all would leave together, and if we all came home together. (*Harbrace* 10a, 10b; *Hodges* 26a, 26b)

CHAPTER 11

Exercise 11–1

1. A healthy social life and participation in sports, experts will tell you, are important parts of an education. 11a (*Harbrace* 11a; *Hodges* 29a)
3. Our school won the basketball championship. 11d (*Harbrace* 11d; *Hodges* 29d)
5. Even though you may fail a course or suffer some setbacks, always keep your goals in sight. 11c (*Harbrace* 11c; *Hodges* 29c)

7. In high school someone checked up on you, in college no one will; a parent or a teacher was usually watching over you, now you're on your own. <u>11g</u> (*Harbrace* 11g; *Hodges* 29g)

9. Academic records and participation in extracurricular activities are both looked at by Admissions Officers when you apply for admission to college. <u>11a</u> (*Harbrace* 11a; *Hodges* 29a)

Exercise 11–2
Answers will vary.

CHAPTER 12

Exercise 12–1
Answers may vary.

1. College, once only for the wealthy, has become available to everyone. <u>12d</u> (*Harbrace* 12d; *Hodges* 30d)

3. You can go either to a state college or to a private college. Although you need more money for the private ones, state schools are less expensive and just as good. <u>12a</u> (*Harbrace* 12a; *Hodges* 30a)

5. Start planning now by choosing a few colleges you like, by getting your recommendations lined up, and by having your high school send a current transcript. <u>12a</u> (*Harbrace* 12a; *Hodges* 30a)

Exercise 12–2
Answers will vary.

Review: Effective Sentences
Answers will vary. Instructors may want to review chapters 8–12 prior to assigning this exercise.

CHAPTER 13

Exercise 13–1
Sentences may vary.

1. <u>ain't, got</u>. He doesn't have any. (*Harbrace* 13c; *Hodges* 19c)

3. <u>Sit</u>. Set that book down on the table. (*Harbrace* 13c; *Hodges* 19c)

5. <u>done, without a blink</u>. She did that without any consideration. (**_Harbrace_ 13b; _Hodges_ 19c**)

7. <u>bottom . . . pitching</u>. Well, your final exam is tomorrow, and you're in trouble if you haven't studied. (**_Harbrace_ 13c; _Hodges_ 19g**)

9. <u>Not</u>. We won't be back here again. (**_Harbrace_ 13b; _Hodges_ 19d**)

Exercise 13–2
Answers will vary.

CHAPTER 14

Exercise 14–1 (_Harbrace_ 14a; _Hodges_ 20a)

1. pinnacle
3. hardy
5. agreed to
7. equitable
9. admission

Exercise 14–2
Sentences can vary.

1. <u>cleanliness is next to godliness</u>. You should shower after playing football, or you won't have much company at dinner. (**_Harbrace_ 14c; _Hodges_ 20c**)

3. <u>better cool it</u>, <u>kick the bucket</u>. The doctor told John to cut down on drinking, and don't drive when he's drinking, or he'd end up dead (or end up a statistic). (**_Harbrace_ 14b; _Hodges_ 20b**)

5. <u>give my eyeteeth</u>, <u>you know, whatever</u>. I would really like to become a (doctor, engineer, executive, etc.) who makes a lot of money. (**_Harbrace_ 14c; _Hodges_ 20c**)

CHAPTER 15

Exercise 15–1
Sentences may vary.

1. Even if you water a new lawn, it could die. (**_Harbrace_ 15a; _Hodges_ 21a**)

3. This week, practice for the big game so you'll be ready and win. (**_Harbrace_ 15c; _Hodges_ 21c**)

5. Just before a football game, you have to psyche yourself into becoming like an animal. (***Harbrace*** 15e; ***Hodges*** 19h)

Exercise 15–2
Sentences may vary.

1. This paragraph is practice in how to write concisely. (***Harbrace*** 15a; ***Hodges*** 21a)
3, 4. Each rule showed you a different method of achieving conciseness, and can help you to write better than you were. (***Harbrace*** 15a, 15c; ***Hodges*** 21a, 21c)
5. You can teach yourself to write better. (***Harbrace*** 15e; ***Hodges*** 19h)

CHAPTER 16

Exercise 16–1
Sentences may vary.

1. Ed is smarter than (Joe, etc.). (***Harbrace*** 16c; ***Hodges*** 22c)
3. He is quick, and his foul shot is good. (***Harbrace*** 16b; ***Hodges*** 22b)
5. That's too much for me to do alone. (***Harbrace*** 16d; ***Hodges*** 22d)
7. Fred and Marie went to the restaurant and ate dinner. (***Harbrace*** 16a; ***Hodges*** 22a)
9. The Packers scored more points than the Patriots. (***Harbrace*** 16c; ***Hodges*** 22c)

Exercise 16–2 (***Harbrace*** 16; ***Hodges*** 22)

My brother and I went to two ballgames last season. The first game that we attended was better, probably because our team won and I almost caught a fly ball. The second game was less eventful, but I did get to eat a hot dog and some of the peanuts they sell in the stands. (My brother ate the rest.) And even though our team didn't win the second game, my brother and I had so much fun, just being together, that we are planning two more trips to the ballpark this season.

Review: Diction
Answers may vary.

CHAPTER 17

Exercise 17–1

1. When you speak, speak clearly. (*Harbrace* 17b; *Hodges* 12b)
3. Those who want to, may write an extra paper. (*Harbrace* 17e; *Hodges* 12e)
5. Her mother, who got the message, called back. (*Harbrace* 17d; *Hodges* 12d)
7. Marie's mother is understanding, responsive, and generous. (*Harbrace* 17c; *Hodges* 12c)
9. The test, which took two hours to finish, wasn't that difficult. (*Harbrace* 17d; *Hodges* 12d)

Exercise 17–2 (*Harbrace* 17; *Hodges* 12, 13)

1. As I see it, college is quite different from high school in many respects, and similar in many others.
3. Your teacher, your counselor, your parents, no one, in fact, is there to stand over you to make you, or remind you to, do your work or take care of your laundry, or make your meals, and so forth.
5. With that in mind, make your own decision about whether to go to college near home or away from home.

CHAPTER 18

Exercise 18–1

1. I like my car, the gas-guzzler. 18c (*Harbrace* 18c; *Hodges* 14c)
3. Some games are high scoring; some games are low scoring. 18a (*Harbrace* 18a; *Hodges* 14a)
5. C (*Harbrace* 18b; *Hodges* 14b)

Exercise 18–2 (*Harbrace* 18a–18c; *Hodges* 14a–14c)

1. The heater in our dormitory room is broken; consequently, we have to bundle up.
3. The readings for this class were written by Toni Morrison, the novelist; Emily Dickinson, the poet; and Tennessee Williams, the playwright.
5. On New Year's Eve, I made two resolutions, exercise and eat right.
7. Today, my English class met in the computer lab; we used the computers to write and send e-mail messages.
9. I broke his favorite coffee mug, the yellow and blue one.

CHAPTER 19

Exercise 19–1

1. That's not his, it's mine. <u>19b</u> (*Harbrace* 19b; *Hodges* 15b)
3. Doesn't she realize she's wrong? <u>19b</u> (*Harbrace* 19b; *Hodges* 15b)
5. Whose brother is it who's making the complaint? <u>19c</u> (*Harbrace* 19c; *Hodges* 15c)
7. The ASPCA's record of helping stray dogs and cats find homes is its best attribute. <u>19a</u> (*Harbrace* 19a; *Hodges* 15a)
9. His grade sheet has three plus's and two minus's. <u>19c</u> (*Harbrace* 19c; *Hodges* 15c)

Exercise 19–2 (*Harbrace* 19a, 19b, 19d; *Hodges* 15a, 15b, 15d)

Stacey and Barbara's favorite pastime is going to the art museum. Stacey's time in the museum is spent studying Monet's and Van Gogh's paintings. She loves the museum's collection of impressionist art. Unlike Stacey, Barbara isn't interested in the Impressionists' work. Barbara spends her time viewing the new exhibits, such as mummies' treasures, women's photography, and '20's memorabilia.

CHAPTER 20

Exercise 20–1

1. C (*Harbrace* 20a; *Hodges* 16a)
3. "Born in the USA" was a hit for The Boss, Bruce Springsteen. <u>20c</u> (*Harbrace* 20c; *Hodges* 16c)
5. C (*Harbrace* 20e; *Hodges* 16e)
7. "Carmela," Marie said, "why don't we go to the movies tonight?" <u>20f</u> (*Harbrace* 20f; *Hodges* 16f)
9. I mean he's stupid, not "intellectually challenged." <u>20d</u> (*Harbrace* 20d; *Hodges* 16d)

Exercise 20–2 (*Harbrace* 20a, 20c–20f; *Hodges* 16a, 16c–16f)

1. He quickly asked, "How do you download a file from the Internet?"
3. Samuel shouted, "How could you leave me here alone!"
5. "When I was younger," he said, "I could easily run 5 miles a day."
7. I would rather stay home and watch "X Files" than go to a movie.
9. Before writing her critique of the short story, Margarita read an essay titled "Imagery in Steinbeck's 'Chrysanthemums.' "

CHAPTER 21

Exercise 21–1

1. Classes begin at 9:00 a.m. on Monday. <u>21a</u> (***Harbrace*** 21a; ***Hodges*** 17a)
3. Holy smoke! That's something. <u>21c</u> (***Harbrace*** 21c; ***Hodges*** 17c)
5. The stadium was just what I thought it would be: large, windy, and expensive. <u>21d</u> (***Harbrace*** 21d; ***Hodges*** 17d)
7. Anyone in this country can (if he or she wants to) become successful. <u>21f</u> (***Harbrace*** 21f; ***Hodges*** 17f)
9. Anytime he [Jim Brown] got the ball, the other team worried. <u>21g</u> (***Harbrace*** 21g; ***Hodges*** 17g)

Exercise 21–2 (***Harbrace*** 21a–21f, h; ***Hodges*** 17a–17f, h)

Recently, my class went to the library to research our essay topics. I had chosen to write about the Internet. But I wasn't sure where to begin my research, so I asked the reference librarian for help. "Excuse me, could you tell me where I might find information on the Internet?" I asked her. She replied, "Are you looking for information that is actually on the Internet or just information about the Internet?" I stood stunned (apparently I needed to think about this a bit more), but soon I decided that information about the Internet—printed or online—would be best.

So, the librarian showed me several helpful periodicals: the *New York Times, Time, Newsweek,* and *Internet World.* She then left me with these final words: "If you need more help after you have narrowed your topic, just let me know." I was able to narrow my topic and find plenty of articles addressing it. Now when I go to the library, I always stop by to say "Hi" to the librarian who helped me.

Review: Punctuation

1. Now that we have covered parts of speech, sentences, and punctuation, you should be prepared, supposedly, to move on to more challenging material, such as paragraphs and essays.
3. If so, be patient.
5. Once that's done, you'll put together paragraphs and essays.
7. Be patient; be persistent.

CHAPTER 22

Exercise 22–1

1. ac-ces'-si'ble	easily approached
3. ac-quire'	to gain possession of
5. ad-vise'	to counsel
7. ben'-e-fit-ed	to be helpful to
9. com'-pe-tence	the state or quality of being competent
11. de-sir'-able	worth seeking
13. ex-ag'-ger-ate	to enlarge disproportionately
15. fas'-ci-nate	to be an object of intense interest to
17. le-git'-i-mate	lawful
19. op-por-tu'-ni-ty	favorable circumstances
21. qui'-et	making no noise
23. sim'-i-lar	showing some resemblance
25. sur-prise'	to encounter suddenly or unexpectedly
27. un-con'-scious	without conscious awareness
29. weath'-er	state of the atmosphere at a given time and place

Exercise 22–2 (*Harbrace* 22b; *Hodges* 18b)

1. compliments
3. guerilla
5. rode, horse
7. peace
9. than
11. patience

Exercise 22–3

1. misunderstand	(*Harbrace* 22c; *Hodges* 18c)
3. reevaluate	(*Harbrace* 22c; *Hodges* 18c)
5. excitable	(*Harbrace* 22d; *Hodges* 18d)
7. writing	(*Harbrace* 22d; *Hodges* 18d)
9. judgment	(*Harbrace* 22d; *Hodges* 18d)
11. defiance	(*Harbrace* 22d; *Hodges* 18d)
13. hungrily	(*Harbrace* 22d; *Hodges* 18d)
15. accompanies	(*Harbrace* 22d; *Hodges* 18d)

Exercise 22–4

1. The ex-captain of the New York Rangers is Mark Messier.
3. It's not as though we live in a high-rise apartment in the city; we're quasi-rural.
5. The people who built the community were hard-boiled immigrants from old-world Europe.

CHAPTER 23

Exercise 23–1

1. He, Don't   (*Harbrace* 23c; *Hodges* 9c)
3. The, Declaration of
   Independence, Americans   (*Harbrace* 23c, 23a; *Hodges* 9c, 9a)
5. Prejudice   (*Harbrace* 23a; *Hodges* 9a)
7. Fox-Five   (*Harbrace* 23a; *Hodges* 9a)
9. War and Peace   (*Harbrace* 23c; *Hodges* 9c)

Exercise 23–2
Sentences may vary. The following rules apply.

1. (*Harbrace* 23b; *Hodges* 9b)
3. (*Harbrace* 23g, 23a(4); *Hodges* 9g, 9a(4))
5. (*Harbrace* 23g; *Hodges* 9g)

CHAPTER 24

Exercise 24–1

1. *Encarta*   (*Harbrace* 24a; *Hodges* 10a)
3. *Bongiorno*   (*Harbrace* 24b; *Hodges* 10b)
5. *did*   (*Harbrace* 24f; *Hodges* 10f)
7. *Pi*   (*Harbrace* 24e; *Hodges* 10e)
9. *Spell Check*   (*Harbrace* 24a; *Hodges* 10a)

Exercise 24–2 (*Harbrace* 24a–24e; *Hodges* 10a–10e)

1. Our public library doesn't subscribe to the *Journal of Behavioral Science* or to the *Washington Post*.
3. I recently watched two documentaries: one about *Brown v. the Board of Education* and another about the sinking of the *Titanic*.
5. I think Kenneth Branaugh's *Hamlet* is much better than the one starring Mel Gibson.
7. Do you prefer to type your papers in *Word* or *WordPerfect*?
9. The new exhibit includes Munch's *The Scream* and Rodin's *The Thinker*.

CHAPTER 25

Exercise 25–1

1. lbs.	(*Harbrace* 25d; *Hodges* 11d)
3. Mr., mtn.	(*Harbrace* 25a, 25d; *Hodges* 11a, 11d)
5. St. Paul, Minn., Apr.	(*Harbrace* 25a, 25b, 25d; *Hodges* 11a, 11b, 11d)
7. $6,500,000 or $6.5 million	(*Harbrace* 25f; *Hodges* 11f)
9. Nov. 25, 1997 or 25 Nov., 1997	(*Harbrace* 25f; *Hodges* 11f)

Review: Capitals, Italics, Abbreviations, Numbers

1. When Marie went to her first English class in college, she was assigned the *Red Badge of Courage*, a novel about the Civil War written by Stephen Crane in the late nineteenth century.
3. At 10:00 the next morning, Dr. Smith gave them a quiz.

Exercise 25–2 (*Harbrace* 25a–25f; *Hodges* 11a–11f)

1. My mother will arrive at 5:00 p.m.
3. I spent $25.10 on a new sweater.
5. On the envelope, I used his home address: 4090 Meadowlark Ave., Camp Hill, PA 17012.
7. Our class reunion will be held on November 16, 1998.
9. Mr. Taylor often watches the NFL games on TV.

CHAPTER 26

Exercise 26–1
Answers will be individual and may vary. Instructors may wish to correct and grade the checklists based on comprehensiveness and adherence to instructions.

CHAPTER 27

Exercise 27–1 (*Harbrace* 27a; *Hodges* 31a)
Answers may vary.

Exercise 27–2 (*Harbrace* 27b; *Hodges* 31b)
Answers may vary.

Exercise 27–3 (*Harbrace* 27b; *Hodges* 31b)
Answers may vary.

CHAPTER 28

Exercise 28–1 (*Harbrace* 28c; *Hodges* 32c)
Answers will vary.

Exercise 28–2 (*Harbrace* 28d, 28e; *Hodges* 32d, 32e)
Answers will vary.

Exercise 28–3 (*Harbrace* 28f, 28g; *Hodges* 32f, 32g)
Answers will vary.

CHAPTER 29

Exercise 29–1
Students should be prepared to turn in the original and revised copies of their essays as well as a paragraph comparing the drafting and revision processes.